Crazy Critter Lady

Crazy Critter Lady

Kelly Meister

The greatness of a nation, and its moral progress, can be judged by the way its animals are treated.

— Mohandas Gandhi

Acknowledgments

Special thanks, first and foremost, to Johnny Moffett, who kept the faith and never stopped believing in me. My heartfelt appreciation to Crystal Ponsor, DVM, Susan Orosz, DVM, and Susan Pontius, DVM, and the great people at South Suburban Animal Hospital, Bird & Exotic Pet Wellness Center, and Brannan Veterinary Clinic, for taking such good care of my ducks. Thanks also to Morri Weaver, DVM, Jill Lloyd, DVM, and the wonderful staff at Anthony Wayne Animal Hospital, for all their years of kindness and generosity. Thank you to Whoville Animal Control Officer Dave, for helping me find all those duck nests! My gratitude to Whoville's Director of Important Things, for keeping the pond fountain running every winter. Many thanks to Terry T. and family for the computer lessons, and for letting me ride Obie. Much gratitude to Bob Tarte for his infinite patience. Thanks and love to John L. Stahl, my partner in crime.

Lastly, thank you Jean Cook. Without whom.

Table of Contents

Table of Contents

Introduction

A lot of people wonder what I do all day. Do I spend whole days tending to critters? Being crazy? Both? In point of fact – and thanks to years of therapy, I'm actually more sane now than I've ever been. Up until a few years ago, my life was darkness and chaos, the result of childhood sexual abuse. But the more time I spent with shrinks, the saner I got. The saner I got, the less inclined I was to spend my time with dysfunctional humans. So I turned to critters instead.

The trouble is that while *I* think I'm pretty level-headed, there are those who disagree. These folks seem to think that it *is* a little crazy to crawl out onto a half-frozen pond to rescue a stranded flightless duck. I got quite a lecture from a therapist for that one! And, many people don't think it's *normal* to carry on conversations with animals. Oh, sure, they'll talk to their pets, but apparently, chatting with chipmunks is taking things a little too far.

I've seen the looks, the raised eyebrows. And I've been on the receiving end of enough lectures on personal safety to know that, because I put the critters first, and take risks most people aren't willing to take, the *perception* is that Kelly's a little nutty. I can live with that.

Do I spend entire days on animal care and rescues? No. I generally take each rescue as it comes: an injured bird here, saving a mouse from my cats there. Weeks and months can pass without a single incident, though there are the daily tasks of caring for cats and ducks.

Mostly, I spend my days coming up with things to do that will get me out of writing. Don't get me wrong – I love nothing better than telling stories. It's the *work* of it that I try to avoid. The hours spent indoors, hunched over a cantankerous computer, when I could be outside playing; the aching shoulders and arthritic hands that would much rather be riding a horse, or working in the garden. And, there's the vexing task of having to switch mental gears. In order to come up with story ideas, it's necessary to shut out my usual cranial activity: How can world peace be achieved in my lifetime? What's good on t.v. tonight? How can I finagle an introduction with George Clooney?

I *like* cluttering my mind and my days with such un-answerable questions. Closing off that pleasant segment of my brain is a bit like busting up a kid's backyard base-ball game for no good reason other than it's bath time. *Rats! Do I hafta?!*

My life is also about healing. Healing the wounds of the past, and learning how to be whole. The critters have helped me with these tasks – in ways I never imagined they could. They've helped by being patient, loving, and trusting, and they've taught me how to be the same. And for those gifts, I owe them. I owe them *big*. It's a debt that I'm happy to spend the rest of my days repaying.

So I'll keep chatting with chipmunks. I'll shoo squirrels out of the road. I'll rescue flightless ducks from frozen ponds. I'll stop to help injured raccoons, and I'll worry about things like rabies later. If that makes me crazy, then so be it.

The Gang

(PART ONE)

I started taking walks down to McKinnon's Pond for two reasons: 1) to dispel cabin fever in winter and 2) to work on my tan in summer. I was told that the distance was a mile, one way, but I never verified this. The distance never really mattered anyway; being out-of-doors, taking the air, *that* was the main thing.

The scenery on this walk left something to be desired. On my right were two sprawling ranch-style apartment complexes designed specifically for the elderly. They were run by a religious organization, and had been optimistically named Eternal Terrace. Just past these was the next stop on the aging tour, a nursing home hiding behind the benign name of Meadow Hall. Few nights went by without paramedics careening past my own apartment, sirens blaring, heading for Meadow Hall: clearly, once you've checked out of there, you've checked out for good.

Beyond the nursing home were apartments for younger folks, and a small business plaza.

On my left, things were more interesting: there was a modest boulevard, with a wide median strip dividing the lanes of traffic. This median had been commendably landscaped many years ago, so that it now contained beautiful mature flowering trees and shrubs. At one point, a stream meanders through it, and many's the time I've seen ducks tending their young in the water, while rabbits snacked on the grass verge beside it.

The focus of this particular subdivision, the communal green space where people were meant to congregate and enjoy life, began just past the business plaza. Clearly, the planners intended three separate but integrated areas: an open meadow, thoughtfully stocked with horseshoe pits, grills, and picnic tables, and divided from the other two areas by way of tall cottonwood trees. Tucked behind the meadow was a small pond well suited to ice skating in winter, and quiet reflection in summer. A children's playground stood sentinel nearby.

Beyond the meadow and small pond lay the main feature, McKinnon's Pond. Nearly three times the size of the small nameless pond and no doubt considerably deeper, McKinnon's Pond served a variety of functions: one end was roped off for swimming (This was regrettable. When I was a child, the City hadn't yet decided to exploit the opportunity to swim in duck-poop-infested waters by charging admission.). At the other end was a boathouse, with paddle boats available for rent (Also regrettable. I once witnessed a fat woman and her equally fat young daughter in one of those boats, chasing a frantic mother duck and her young while I stood at water's edge shouting obscenities at them. Eventually, those cruel people backed off, though they didn't capsize and drown, as I had hoped.).

The rest of the pond was given over to occasional rescue drills conducted by the Fire Department, father and son fishing derbies, and the resident duck population. Along the banks were strategically placed benches, trees, and still more picnic tables. If you could ignore the existence of the interstate highway located mere yards away from the pond (and the occasional honks from passing truckers as they eyeballed bikini-clad young ladies on the beach), McKinnon's Pond could be a pleasant place indeed.

The ducks certainly thought so. Despite their migratory nature, a number of mallards chose to weather the weather, as it were, and make the pond their year-round home. Joining them were three extra-large ducks – two white fellows and a female with mallard markings. I would later learn that these three (*Pekins* and *Rouens,* or domestic ducks, generally intended for farm life, as they are incapable of flight) had been dumped at the pond when they stopped being cute little ducklings.

The domestic ducks were hard to ignore. Despite logic which dictated that they stay on the far side of the pond where people seldom went, these ducks chose to hang out in surprising proximity to the human element. This turned out to be a wise choice: I often saw people pausing in their walks to feed them. Eternal Terracers would slowly make their way to the pond with a sack of bread; a fifty-ish couple returned time and again with a small bag.

That couple would stand on the bank and toss handfuls of the contents, and the big ducks would come right up and pick pieces off the tops of their shoes! My curiosity got the best of me, and after watching a few of these adventures in duck feeding, I approached the couple, asking what was in their bag and where to get it. From then on, I brought my own bag of cracked corn. Sitting on a bench, I'd be surrounded by a sea of brave and greedy ducks.

The three large ones were the greediest. The two white fellows stood tall and brave enough to crane their necks and steal the corn that would spill onto the bench. Bread, their special treat, had to be guarded zealously against just this sort of thievery. The large brown duck – clearly afraid of humans – would shy away from the proffered bread: as far as Missy Miss (as I dubbed her) was concerned, if it wasn't on the ground, she wasn't eating it. What *was* on the ground, she Hoovered up like a vacuum cleaner, shouldering smaller ducks out of the way so she could have even more.

I was surprised by how quickly feeding the ducks became addictive, but the ducks themselves had a hand in that. As they came to recognize me, they began a routine which continues to this day: the first duck to make visual contact with me begins to quack. This gets the others looking and quacking, and the next thing you know, twenty-odd ducks are waddling, en mass, in my direction. It's the duck equivalent of the family dog's joyful dance when you walk in the door, and it thoroughly warms my heart every time they do it.

It came as a further surprise – and shouldn't have – to realize that after I moved a few miles away and no longer approached on foot, the ducks learned to recognize the color of my car. The quacking often began before I even got out.

It must be said that I wasn't actually *looking* for friendship with a gang of ducks. Let's face it, they're boring animals, right? Well, yes and no. The wild mallards, with their inherent reserve, seemed to have no personalities whatsoever. While as many as twenty of them would join the feeds, I was unable to distinguish one ounce of charisma in any of them. The domestics were another matter entirely.

What the domestics lacked in survival instincts, they more than made up for with cheerful natures. *Yay, you're here!*, they seemed to say. None among them carried cell phones, not a one had children in a traveling soccer league, and no one held a job. They had all day to do nothing more than simply *be,* a thing that appealed to my normally-chaotic mind.

As a writer, and as a matter of personal choice, I live a fairly isolated life; the less time I spend with humans, the better I get along with them. But critters are another story: they have no hidden agendas, they're incapable of being dishonest, and if you treat them well, they will bestow upon you their unconditional love.

Having grown up in a family where love was conditioned on keeping silent and maintaining the status quo, the no-strings-attached affection offered up by those ducks was better medicine than anything the pharmaceutical companies could invent. So I frequently chose to linger, and before long I found myself thoroughly enmeshed in the lives of those goofy characters.

One of God's Own

It was late morning on a fine sunny fall day, and I'd just spent a pleasant thirty minutes down at the pond with the ducks. I was no more than a quarter-mile from home and driving in that direction when I passed a raccoon sitting on his haunches by the side of the road. What were the odds, I mused, of an animal being struck by a car and killed, then landing on his haunches? A small voice in my head whispered that perhaps he wasn't dead, and with this thought, I pulled off the road. Before I approached the critter, I reached into the trunk of my car for the snow shovel that resides there.

Some years ago, it began to grieve me deeply to see the end result of man's thoughtless encroachment on creature habitat: it seemed that more and more animals every year were meeting gruesome and untimely deaths on area roads. So I carried the shovel in my car. When I was able to pull off the road safely, and when the critter corpse was still three-dimensional, I shoveled it off the road and said a small prayer to the Gods, asking that this unfortunate animal be given special consideration in the Hereafter. Holding the shovel now, I approached the raccoon.

There wasn't time to stop and think. I mean, what do *you* do in an emergency? Most of us switch to autopilot, where instinct takes over, and conscious thought seems to get put on hold. Rabies never crossed my mind. There *was* one fleeting thought, a vague memory of my friend Sam lecturing me on the dangers of being bitten, but I shrugged it away: if you spend too much time worrying about what *could* happen, nothing much actually gets done.

I suppose that in the case of a potentially dangerous animal, many people *would* give the matter some thought first – if they bothered to think at all. It's worth noting that no one driving by that day stopped to help, or even slowed down. *It's just a raccoon.* But to me, he was someone in need of help, so instead of pausing to consider the risks, or whether the poor creature was worthy of my assistance, I let autopilot take over: *help now, think later.*

I gently slipped the shovel under his hind end. I wanted to move him further away from the road, but he was quite heavy and as I made a second attempt, he slowly spread his front legs, trying to brace himself against this intrusive movement. I stopped my efforts and considered the situation. Easily weighing twenty pounds or better, showing no outward sign of injury but giving every indication of mental – and, no doubt, other internal injuries as well, something clearly had to be done. He was much too close to the road for my liking, and there was no doubt in my mind that eventually, some sick person would come along and see an opportunity for a little vehicular target practice.

In a mild panic, my mind racing but getting nowhere, I tried once more to shovel the raccoon to safety. As I did, he slowly turned his head in an effort to get a look at the stranger behind him. Indeed: I'd been so intent on the rescue that I hadn't bothered to tell him about it. I leaned into his view and said softly, "It's just me, little guy, I'm going to help you." I realized that the tools I needed for the job were in my house, just up the road. Reluctant to leave the poor fellow, but having no alternatives at hand, I told him I'd be right back, and ran to my car. I stomped on the gas pedal, careening up the street and into the driveway. I raced through the house gathering equipment, threw it all into the car and sped back to the raccoon. To my relief, no one had bothered him while I was gone.

I announced my return before I set the laundry basket down beside him. Putting on my heavy suede gardening gloves – the ones I used when handling rose bushes – I pulled from the car a thick woolen afghan I'd knitted years before and made the mistake of putting through the washer and dryer. There was now no more densely-knitted afghan anywhere in the world. I draped the blanket around the raccoon's shoulders, then gingerly picked him up under his armpits. I thought that between the thick gloves and the thick afghan, he wasn't likely to do much damage should he manage a bite. He didn't even try.

As I eased him into the basket, he reached out one front paw and grasped the basket's edge. I gently released the paw and settled him in, covering him with the remainder of the blanket. He never struggled, or even cried out.

I drove quickly to the nearest veterinarian – a man who was located about a mile from my home. My mind drew a momentary blank when I found the doors locked, and then the panic started in earnest. There was no question but that the raccoon needed euthanized – the sooner the better. I'd seen enough animals in shock to know that he was, too, and the fact that he hadn't even tried to defend himself against me merely served to underscore the severity of his condition. My mission, therefore, was to get him euthanized as soon as possible. I had no way of knowing, as I sped off toward Vet #2, how very nearly impossible that would prove to be.

Vet #2, Dr. Green, had been treating my cats for years. And while most of his staff had been working there as long as I'd been going, one woman came to stand out from the others. Sam was a veterinary technician with a touch of critter fever all her own. We traded endless animal stories whenever I was in the office. Our friendship eventually expanded to include dinners at a local Mexican restaurant, and visits to her country home, where I became familiar with a large indoor/outdoor brood of rescued dogs, cats, and the occasional duckling. Rounding out her menagerie was Obie the horse.

It was Sam who told me about the shovel-in-the-trunk trick, Sam who doled out the occasional lecture on the dangers of rabies, Sam who had given me free food and drugs for my cats when she knew I was struggling financially. And it was Sam's God I frequently railed against when animals needlessly suffered.

Sam and I had profound ideological differences, and there were times when those differences threatened to derail our friendship. Sam bore my outbursts with more patience and grace than I probably deserved, a fact for which I am eternally grateful. The thing that always carried the day was our mutual love of critters, and I could've used her help now in dealing with the raccoon. Unfortunately, she couldn't be reached.

Among Dr. Green's myriad responsibilities, he euthanized the wild animals caught by the city he worked in. Being savvy enough to know how red tape worked, I was thoroughly prepared to lie through my teeth and say I had found the raccoon in his city, instead of mine. Only problem was, he wasn't in the office, and wouldn't be until Monday morning. I was told that his associate, Dr. Jill – a woman whom I liked very much – wouldn't do the job. The staff weren't even prepared to phone her at home (where she'd gone for lunch) and ask. Evidently, Dr. Jill preferred to work only on cute, fuzzy puppies and kitties. Sam told me later that if she had been working that day, she'd have either guilted Dr. Jill into doing the procedure, or quite possibly have done it herself - either of which would have been fine with me but were not options at the time.

Seeing the panic on my face, and knowing me well enough to know that I wouldn't be dissuaded, the staff began making phone calls to see who, among the area's veterinarians, was working on Saturday, and would euthanize a raccoon. They finally found one, and I hurried out the door and sped down the road.

Before the laundry basket and I were even fully in the door, the girl behind the desk asked if I had come from Dr. Green's office. Answering in the affirmative, I was told that they weren't licensed to handle a raccoon, a fiction that I only learned later was a fiction, designed to avoid having to deal with a wild – and potentially dangerous – animal. I set the basket on the floor, off to the side of the front desk. Someone looking at it would have thought that it contained a large blanket and nothing else. There hadn't been any movement at all the entire time it was in my car, so rather sarcastically, I asked if they were licensed to look and see whether the raccoon was still alive. He was.

It was suggested that I call the City and have them handle the matter. Exasperated, I explained that the City took its animals to Dr. Green – from whose office I had just come. "Look," I said as patiently as I could manage, "I can't just take him home and let him suffer until Monday. He needs euthanized *now*." The desk girl then suggested Wild Haven Nursery, a local wildlife rehab center that did wonderful work but rarely answered their phone. I stood by while she placed the call.

The first thing Wild Haven Nursery wanted to know was where the raccoon had been found. "*Here*," I answered tersely, "in the city we're in!" Unable to fob it off as *sorry-wrong-city-we-can't-help-you*, it was concluded that the Nursery handled virtually every animal that God created – except raccoons. They suggested that we try the Park Rangers. Whose voice mail the desk girl reached and left a message.

A staff technician had been lurking in the lobby, monitoring the girl's progress. Hearing that her efforts had come to naught, the Tech stood staring at the floor for a few minutes, seeming to consider something. At length, she looked up at me and made a small furtive gesture with her hand. Before she could change her mind, I picked up the basket and followed her to an exam room.

The Tech took another look under the blanket and told me that they would want to sedate the raccoon first, as a precaution. It would be ten-odd minutes before the sedative took effect, did I want to come back later for my belongings? "No," I answered firmly, "I'll wait in the lobby." Things rarely take as long as claimed, when folks know you're waiting nearby.

There had been a woman in the lobby watching the proceedings who told me, in the midst of the phone calls, what a "really nice thing" I was doing. I had responded flatly that *I* knew I was doing a nice thing, but I couldn't seem to find anyone to help me. And indeed, waiting those final minutes, the frustration caught up with the panic, and I found myself very near to tears.

In less time than she said it would take, the Tech came out with my basket and blanket. She informed me that the raccoon was gone, and had passed quickly and painlessly. I was told that I owed no money for either the procedure or disposal of the body – jolly decent of them, actually – then I thanked them all and left. The tears began to flow before I'd even left the parking lot. They continued the entire drive home.

One animal, one of God's creatures, one raccoon so injured that he hadn't put up any kind of fight, had needed help. One shot of Pentobarbital to end his suffering, and *not one* veterinarian – all of whom had spent eight years in medical school, presumably because they loved animals – *not one* had been willing to help. They'd had to be pushed and prodded, and they'd been forced to contend with a woman who refused to take 'no' for an answer, when all they'd really wanted was to pass the problem on to someone else. I was deeply disgusted. I despaired. And I lost a large measure of respect for the vets involved.

In the midst of all those tears I shed, I said a prayer – *wailed* a prayer - to the Gods to please tell that poor raccoon that in his life, there *was* one person who loved him, even if it was only in his final hour.

I hope They were listening.

In an effort to stave off the wave of depression I felt building, I forced myself to go for a walk at the local park. While I'd been chasing veterinarians, the sun had turned to clouds, and it was beginning to sprinkle. I walked the trail blindly, more for something to do than with actual purpose.

Because of the rain, I had the park to myself. Enjoying the feel of the solitude, I completed one full circuit of the loop trail. As I rounded a curve in the path, I looked up to see five deer looking back at me. As they studied me, it was clear that they, too, had believed they'd had the park to themselves.

I like deer. I like their soft, soulful eyes. I like the way they size me up, conclude that I'm harmless, and go back to their grazing. I like that they can *sense* harmlessness in me. And they might've sensed it in me this day, as well, but for the rising wind that made my umbrella flail about. With one wide-eyed glance at the billowing entity, all five deer took off at once, galloping across the meadow toward the woods.

As I watched them go, I realized that the Gods *had* been listening: what better way to relieve the sorrow of death than to show me the beauty of life?

Winkie

His name was William Wallace, but owing to his exceptionally large round eyes, which would blink at me guilelessly, he came to be known as Winkie; *Willie*, if he was being bad. He and his siblings had been left in a box outside Dr. Green's office. The staff had cleaned them up, attended to matters of vaccinations and neutering, and offered them for sale for ten dollars each. The guy I'd been living with – and was on the verge of leaving – adopted the scrawny grey tabby after Winkie charmed him by climbing up his arm and perching on his shoulder. Once ensconced in our home, though, the little fellow became the Kitten From Hell, and the walls fairly echoed with shouts of, "*Willie!*"

The about-to-be-ex boyfriend had no concept of instilling rules and discipline in young animals, and his *no*'s might just as well have been *yes*'s. Winkie would climb right up on to our chairs, our table, our *dinner plates*, and the man would merely say 'no.' I, on the other hand, emphasized every shouted "*NO!*" by picking kitty up and depositing him firmly on the floor. When I tired of the battle, I shut him up in the attic.

After dinner, I would open the attic door to an unexpected sight: Winkie lying quietly at the top step, looking down at me with surprising calm; I had assumed that he would be bouncing off the walls, yowling. Instead, he would sedately descend the stairs and be an adorable kitten – until the next meal. He seemed to have selective hearing, with an impeccable ability to filter out the word 'no.' But there was something else, as well.

I sent the boyfriend packing, assuming that he would take his cat with him. Much to my surprise, he told me to keep the kitten, saying that he didn't think Winkie would be happy with him. I was only too glad to agree. The house was quieter, then, but not for the reason you might think. It became quieter because almost immediately after the boyfriend left, Winkie settled down and began to mind his manners; I didn't have to shout at him anymore. He still managed to get into plenty of kitten trouble – I once caught him trying to eat a paper clip – but it was of a tolerable variety, and didn't interfere with my meals.

He wrought havoc on Muffin. I had only recently adopted her and, judging from her behavior, it was obvious that she'd spent her formative years in the company of a rather fussy old lady: she hadn't been allowed on furniture, and she certainly hadn't mingled with other cats. Now, here she was being forced to share her home with an aggravating kitten who once did *something*

(I don't know what, I was out of the room) which resulted in a slice in her ear that remains to this day.

Winkie first showed his cheeky nature during just such an encounter with Muffin. I was engaged in some kitchen activity when I heard her growling in the next room. Without even bothering to investigate, I issued a warning, "Willie? Are you being bad? It would *behoove* you to be good!" To which a puzzled voice replied, "I don't have hooves, Kelly!" I knew then that he would always be a pleasant handful.

Our home at that time was the upper floor of a duplex overlooking a river. The back door opened out onto a small landing, where I would sit most mornings with a cup of tea and enjoy the view. The cats liked it, too, although Winkie was more interested than I cared in descending the stairs to explore the rest of the world. As they were both strictly indoor cats, I didn't encourage his explorations; I didn't want him getting too comfortable outdoors. When we moved to the ground-floor apartment near McKinnon's Pond some months later, though, I got to thinking about how much he had enjoyed those brief outings.

The new home was about a mile up the road from the pond and its ducks, and I got it into my head that Winkie might like to see them. So I bought a harness and leash, and set about teaching him to go for walks. It required a patience I didn't know I possessed. Winkie was a jumpety cat, and entirely unused to everyday things like people, traffic, and being hindered by a leash.

Our first attempts were halting and brief: I would pick him up and carry him across the grass to the sidewalk, and he would walk from the sidewalk directly back to our door. Eventually, though, his curiosity found him, and he began to follow the sidewalk to see where it led.

It led to some pretty interesting places indeed: to the row of shrubs where he'd seen rabbits run; to the grounds of Eternal Terrace; to the gravel path by the stream; to the brick wall that he came to love for its "I'm king of the world" possibilities; to the catnip plants growing wild and inviting. What an exciting world it was!

He'd had to go to the vet, that summer. I noticed him panting, open-mouthed, and had been concerned. Winkie was diagnosed with asthma and given a pill to take every day, and that seemed to be the end of the matter. In the meantime, he had an extraordinary walk around Eternal Terrace.

I had reached the conclusion, early on, that Winkie was never going to walk down to McKinnon's Pond. There were just too many scary things along the way: a street frequented by cars, children on bicycles, too many open spaces where he would feel uncomfortably vulnerable. He didn't seem to care about what he was missing, anyway, so I contented myself with the knowledge that he thoroughly enjoyed our walks just the way they were. As it turned out, we didn't need to go all the way to the pond to see ducks, after all.

We were taking our usual meandering stroll one day, which led us to Eternal Terrace. It really was a pretty place, pleasantly landscaped, with a creek running through it. Some of the more energetic residents planted flowers around their patios, and I was admiring just such a flower bed this day. I stood chatting with the gardener responsible and as we talked, Winkie grew bored. I picked him up just about the time the lady went back inside her home – and just about the time the mama duck and two ducklings emerged from the underbrush by the creek and walked toward the parking lot we were standing in.

They walked in formation, one baby duck behind the other, with mama bringing up the rear. I swear she was quacking a quiet cadence to them. They passed within ten feet of us – I, holding Winkie in my arms and whispering softly, "Birdies, Winkie! *Big* birdies!" and Winkie resting calmly on his perch, watching the parade with interest. We remained that way for some minutes, the breeze blowing gently while the sun shone down on us. Mama and her young made their way to a row of shrubs and disappeared, I set Winkie back down on the ground, and we resumed our walk. It had been a magical moment.

That summer was packed with just such moments, though they wouldn't all be duck-filled. When it was too hot to walk during the day, we'd go late at night. Winkie enjoyed the evenings more – he seemed to feel safer under cover of darkness and shadow. He would visit all of his daytime haunts, and we discovered a new one, as well: another area of lawn on the Eternal Terrace grounds, where a security light blazed all night, attracting hundreds of flying insects. One night, as Winkie led me through the grass, I was startled when he leapt up as high as my head to catch a bug.

During the winter, it was generally too cold and snowy to be outside for any length of time, and our walks had to be suspended until spring. Winkie made his wishes known any number of times by picking up the leash in his mouth, carrying it across the floor and leaving it where I couldn't help but notice. I was warmed as much by his intelligence as I was by his desire to continue our adventures.

He had an increasing number of asthma attacks, that winter. I'd had to take him to the all-night emergency vet several times, which was no small thing. Apart from the fact that Winkie didn't like riding in cars, the all-night vet was located a good fifteen miles away. In the midst of a cold, dark, panicked night, it seemed much farther. One of his attacks was so severe, they'd had to put him in an oxygen tank for a time, but it seemed to make the difference, and I remained oblivious to the increasing seriousness of his condition. Mind you, it wasn't out of negligence; I didn't realize the severity of the problem because no one else did, either.

That spring, we resumed our walks. I would rattle the metal bits on Winkie's harness and say, "Let's go see things!" He would race into the room, purring and chirruping at the same time, and hold himself still so I could attach the harness and leash, then out the door we went. We had become something of an item in the neighborhood: more than once, around town, I had been approached with the question, "Aren't you the lady who walks her cat?" I never realized that we'd had an audience.

Winkie expressed his gratitude for our adventures in the most obvious way he could think of. At least once during every single walk, I would tell him, "I'm ever so proud of you, my big, brave, adventure cat!" As I said it, I would bend down to run my hand over his head. Winkie would rear up on his hind legs and head-butt that hand in mid-air. The gesture was unmistakable, and the fact

that he even concerned himself with expressing gratitude filled my heart with love.

One morning that summer, I awoke to find Winkie
lying on my bed, panting from another asthma attack –
except that this wasn't 'another' attack, it was the same
one he'd had the night before. I had taken him, in the
wee small hours, to the all-night vet, who had done what
she could. I assumed it was enough, but clearly, he was
in distress. I loaded him into his carrier and drove to Dr.
Green's office.

Dr. Green would need time to deal with the problem, so I left Winkie there. Not long after I drove home,
though, Dr. Green called to say that Winkie's condition had worsened and the situation didn't look good.
I raced to my car and stepped on the gas as the tears
began to flow.

Several times that year, I had remarked to friends
that I hoped Winkie's condition wouldn't reach a point
where I would have to "make a decision" – meaning
euthanize. I'd said it carelessly, with the nonchalance of
one who has no idea how close to the mark she is. Now, I
realized as I drove back to Dr. Green's, now I *would* have
to make that decision.

When I arrived, Dr. Green told me that he'd taken
an x-ray, which showed scar tissue on Winkie's lungs,
and fluid around his heart. In the meantime, owing
to the stress of being somewhere that frightened him,
Winkie's attack had gone into overdrive. Dr. Green had
done everything in his power to rein it in, from steroids to oxygen. By the time I got there, Winkie actually
looked pretty good, but Dr. Green kept talking about
that x-ray.

I couldn't get my mind around what he was saying. I suppose I thought that he could fix the problem, and I was waiting for him to present some treatment options. Instead, he started telling me about his Aunt Somebody, and how she had suffered from a similar illness. Her quality of life, he remarked, had been nonexistent.

Through a fog, I asked blankly, "You think Winkie is suffering?" Dr. Green said yes. I looked at Winkie, who was lying quietly on the table, a staffer holding a tube of oxygen under his nose. He was watching with interest a rather large dog that a couple of assistants were trying to wrestle into submission. He didn't *look* like he was suffering, but Dr. Green didn't talk about this sort of thing without a good reason – a reason I didn't understand at the time, but acknowledged all the same. "Well," I replied in a daze, "then we should probably euthanize."

Dr. Green nodded, then set about gathering what he needed. He spent such an inordinate amount of time getting his supplies together that it took me a few minutes to realize he was giving me time to say good-bye. I spent that time bent over my beloved Winkie, whispering through my tears how much I loved him, how much I would miss him. How proud of him I was. "I'll love you forever, Winkel, my sweet boy." And then he was gone. Peacefully. Painlessly. Forever.

I drove home in tears, closed all my apartment windows, sat down on the bed and *howled*. For several hours. I had euthanized pets before, but I had never had to make a life-or-death decision on such short, unexpected notice. I cried so hard, that day, for so long, that my sinuses swelled shut, and remained that way for several days after.

Winkie's death threw me into a tailspin of depression, the like of which I was already plenty familiar with. A life-long sufferer, I'd spent several years as a lab rat while various doctors tried various medications on me – all of which ultimately produced horrific side-effects. I became so disgusted by the drugs' lack of success that I finally elected to deal with the problem of depression med-free.

Trying to get a decent night's sleep, though, was a battle without end. In sheer desperation, I consulted yet another doctor, who made the bold suggestion that I consider trying an anti-psychotic drug to regulate my sleep. "Will it *make* me psychotic?" I asked, rather hoping that it would. The doctor assured me that the drug would do nothing more than quiet the noise in my head, and in this, she was correct: even in the darkest depths of grief for Winkie, I was finally able to sleep. But sleep was the easy part.

My grief was compounded by my surroundings: the brick wall he loved to walk the length of, the trees and shrubs we explored in the dead of night. Here, there, and everywhere were reminders of our adventures, the very walks that had solidified the bond between us. For a long time after Winkie's death, simply leaving my home was excruciatingly painful.

He came to me once, months later. Relaxed, in the midst of a massage, I heard his sing-song voice in my head. He didn't understand my grief, and my sorrow troubled him.

I wanted more time, Winkie.
Greedy, Kelly!
Yes, Winkie, I was greedy.
Always with you, Kelly!

Thankfully, he didn't understand that he'd been entitled to more than the three short years he'd gotten. That was my painful secret, and I wasn't about to share it with him.

My friend Sam, who had had that awful day off work, looked into the matter the minute she got wind of it. She told me later that she'd seen the x-ray, that it looked like Winkie had had the lungs of an old man who'd suffered from emphysema his entire life. Dr. Green felt that Winkie had actually had an auto-immune disease which settled in his heart and lungs. There was nothing anyone could have done.

Dr. Green sent a card of condolence – a customary practice these days. In addition to his words of sympathy was his expressed conviction that my decision to euthanize had been "correct and kind." Looking out over our formerly glorious empire, my grieving heart felt neither.

When I was a young child, my father killed a neighbor's cat in front of me. The act was intentional: there were secrets he wished me to keep. My memories of that incident are mercifully vague, but the horror, and the agony, remain vivid through the decades. In addition, I carry with me a childishly naïve sense of guilt that I might have somehow saved that cat, but didn't.

So it was with Winkie, as well, and the devastation was complete: Why didn't I see that Winkie's condition was getting worse? Why did I think a mere pill once a day would take care of the problem? Why? Why? Why?

It is, of course, the unanswerables that will eat away at your soul, if you let them. For many years, I did.

The Gang

(PART TWO)

The summer that I started feeding the ducks in earnest, I bought a point-and-shoot camera with a zoomy feature. I could zoom in on the ducklings who were still afraid to come close, and I could back the lens off for wide shots of my sea of ducks. But the real genius was in the idea to sit down on the ground among them; it proved to be the gesture that cemented our friendship. Up on the bench, I towered over them like a benign feeding machine. Down at their level, I became as one of them. Not only did I have a duck's-eye view of things, but I appeared considerably less threatening to them, as well.

Over time, as they became accustomed to the new arrangement, they took to circling around behind me. It gave the more cautious among them the additional comfort of being out of my line of sight, and there was the added bonus of finding chunks of bread spilling out of the bag.

There were several duck moms, that summer, but Missy Miss was not among them. None of the ducks were particularly good mothers: they frequently abandoned their young out in the middle of the pond in favor of a meal with me, resulting in groups of distressed ducklings *peep-peeping* in a frantic attempt to locate mama. Every day that I visited, there would be fewer ducklings than the time before – typical, I learned, as the area was rife with predators.

I've never cared much for the concept of survival of the fittest. I think *every* critter should have a fair shot at life. Feeling frustrated and helpless, there were times when I complained loudly to Sam that, "Nature *sucks!*" Since I was powerless to do anything about the disappearing ducklings, though, I was forced to resign myself to its inevitability.

The ducklings themselves were nothing short of adorable. Tiny little puffballs who weighed so little that they seemed to walk on water, the babies were always the most excited to see me coming. They used my approach as an excuse to race each other, to see who could get there first. It never really mattered who won – the chase was the thing.

They would maintain a discreet distance from me, working the outer edges of the crowd. The adult ducks felt no compunction about nipping the babies, or otherwise pushing them out of the way, which made the young understandably cautious. In every group, though, there was always one tenacious baby whose attitude belied his tiny stature.

This little guy would get hold of a chunk of bread – always slightly bigger than his bill could comfortably handle – and, determined to keep his prize, would race around the fringes of the crowd, some greedy adult hot on his heels. Invariably, Big Duck would lose interest in the chase, and Baby would wrestle his prize into the water to soften it up before he ate it. On the sidelines, I would quietly cheer him on.

The babies' *peep-peeping* struck a maternal chord in me. High-pitched, and strongly resembling a chick's *cheep*, it had a heart-rending quality to it that inspired in me a fierce protectiveness. Any number of times, I got cross with people who allowed their unleashed dogs to pass by too closely. I knew the ducks would come back out of the water once the dogs had left, but that wasn't the point. *Do you not see us sitting here having a quiet interlude?* I always wondered of the careless owners. I often had to remind myself that this was, in fact, a public park, and not my private game reserve.

As the babies grew, their voices deepened, until *peep-peep* became *churp-churp*. By the end of the summer, they would get their Quack. Their wings seemed to take longer to catch up. I had to smile as I watched them at water's edge, bathing and grooming their feathers as they'd seen mama do, and flapping tiny appendages no larger than your thumb, and clearly thinking themselves Very Big Ducks indeed!

Toward the end of summer, when the babies' size very nearly matched the adults, I could no longer distinguish who was who. It was always a relief when they reached a size that made them unlikely as prey: if a baby duck made it to September, chances were very good that he would make it to adulthood.

I brought Sam with me once to feed the ducks, that summer. We sat on the bank in the gathering dusk tossing handfuls of corn when a mama with six young joined us – a mama I hadn't seen before. Apparently, she and her young had been hiding out somewhere on the pond and, for whatever reason, chose this evening to make their first appearance.

What was more surprising than their existence was the fact that we were, apparently, already acquainted: both mama and the ducklings came within inches of me, weaving in and out between my outstretched legs, seemingly unconcerned about the hulking mass of human sprawled before them. I glanced at my friend and remarked, "I don't know who this mama is," to which she replied with a smile, "She knows *you*!"

This was the payoff for me: not seas of ducks, or enthusiastic quacking masses, but the simple fact of their *trust*. There would always be a boundary that I would not be welcome to cross; they were, after all, wild animals. But inasmuch as they were able, as long as I respected the rules (no loud noises, no sudden moves, and for most, no touching), they were willing to put a measure of their faith in me. It was a treasured and priceless gift.

Zoë the Barky Dog

In addition to my walk down to the pond, I had a second route which took me through a different neighborhood. The route was a two-mile loop that I enjoyed for exactly the features my duck walk didn't have: houses. Houses with yards, and people outside doing yard-related things. Because of those yards, and the regularity of my walks, I made a number of acquaintances along the way.

About halfway along the route, there was a house on a corner lot. I would walk past the front of the house, then turn the corner and pass the side and back yard of that house. The back yard in question was enclosed by a chain-link fence, and contained within was a very barky yellow lab.

She raced up and down behind the fence, barking to beat the band, virtually every time I walked by. Her commentary was often punctuated by great leaps into the air and, periodically, she felt sufficiently moved to stand on her hind legs, her front paws resting on top of the fence like a preacher's hands on a pulpit, and broadcast from on high. At the time, I had no idea what she was saying, only that she was saying it very emphatically indeed.

This display of canine might went on for several months. I glimpsed enough of the yard to see that she had access to the family garage – probably where her food and water were, and the yard itself was hers to play in. And while I knew for a fact that people actually lived there, I rarely saw any evidence to indicate their day-to-day presence, so that it appeared to the untrained eye that the dog had been left to her own devices. The untrained eye turned out to be right.

On one of the rare occasions that I saw dog and humans in the same place at the same time, I heard the man call her Zoë. *Interesting name for a dog*, I mused. Several days later, during the usual display of doggy brawn, I caught her off-guard by admonishing, "Zoë! You big barky dog!" The transformation was sudden and funny: she stopped in mid-leap *and* mid-bark, pulled her head back on her shoulders, and managed a sort of, "Rowf? Do I know you?" "Silly girl," I announced, then turned and walked on. For the first time, she remained silent.

It quickly became clear to me that Zoë hadn't been protecting life and limb after all. She'd been asking for attention. Loudly. Repeatedly. Because apparently, she wasn't getting much of it from her humans. The day I figured that out was the day I approached the fence for a visit. Zoë was so relieved, she whined.

And so began an association that would continue through all seasons. Sometimes Zoë would bring me a tennis ball to throw for her, and I was happy to oblige.

Most often, she would stand on her hind legs, propping herself up against the fence with her front paws, and ask me for a pet and a scratch. Judging from the way she always smelled, I guessed she wasn't allowed inside the house much. It broke my heart.

Despite the fact that I owned no dogs of my own, I took to buying cheap dog biscuits at the grocery store. Before I set out on my walks, I would load my pockets, and distribute the spoils thusly: half at the beginning of the walk, and half as I passed by again on my way home.

The street from where I accessed Zoë's yard was a curved one, and from the other end of that curve – a block or so away – I could just see Zoë sitting at the fence, watching for my return. It usually took me thirty minutes to complete the loop. I have no way of knowing whether Zoë waited there for me the whole time, or whether she had an internal clock to tell her to stop chasing the squirrels and go back to the fence. When I'd get half-way down that curved street and was close enough for Zoë to be sure it was me, the dance would begin: prancing back and forth, throwing in a leap or two, she let me know how glad she was to see me again so soon – and all without a single bark; those noisy days were over.

It was during the rare occasions when Zoë was allowed to keep her humans company out in the front yard that her owners became aware of our relationship: Zoe would spot me walking up the sidewalk and race out to greet me, unhindered by the backyard fence. The humans never said anything about the biscuits they saw me give her – in fact, they never said much of anything at all, but I got a vibe that the man might be a little annoyed by the obvious affection between Zoë and I.

My suspicion was confirmed the day he appeared and told me that he wanted me to cut back on the biscuits. It wasn't out of concern for her mildly excessive weight, you understand. No, what the man *said* was that Zoë didn't seem to mind him very well on those occasions when I was in the vicinity. What I *heard* was, "Stop being so nice to my dog." "No problem," I said. *Screw you*, I thought.

That the man was annoyed by our friendship was unfathomable to me – a man who couldn't even be bothered to bathe his smelly dog. How petty! What a creep! I walked away from that encounter chewing on all sorts of expletives that never got said. Mostly, I felt bad for Zoë. She deserved a better family than this – people who were rarely home, but yet begrudged those who reached out to their lonely dog.

There was only one solution: keep spoiling her as best I could. It was easy enough to figure out that the man and his wife worked banker's hours, with weekends off, so I simply altered the days and times I took my walks to suit the times when Zoë's humans would most likely be gone.

We carried on much as before, my pockets loaded with biscuits, and Zoë always glad of a pet and a scratch. When I moved a few miles away, the walks became very infrequent, and I went several months without seeing her until, one crisp fall day, I rounded the corner and saw one very happy yellow lab prancing quietly behind a fence.

Mouse in the House

I live in a converted chicken coop. This is significant only because the conversion took place several decades ago and, since that time, the place has suffered from a grievous case of neglect. Walls are out of kilter, you could roll a marble down the slope that is the kitchen floor, doors no longer close flush with the jamb. And while it must be said that the house has considerable personality in spite of the deficiencies, I knew when I moved in that I would be sharing my new home with a larger cast of characters than just my three cats.

I suspected that we had a boarder when Buddy started spending an inordinate amount of time in the laundry room. Spanky soon joined him, and the two of them would take up positions – Buddy on top of the dryer, Spanky in the litter box – facing a small hole in the wall. If I couldn't find either cat elsewhere in the house, I knew to look for them at Checkpoint Charlie.

Occasionally, Muffin joined the vigils, but being older, and considerably more dignified, she generally found hanging around waiting for mice to appear beneath her. She *did* have a proud history of catching rodents at the apartment near McKinnon's Pond. I would let her out for some supervised air-taking and she'd dash under the shrubs, reappearing later with some small gray creature that had apparently done little more than just stand there and let her catch him.

She would toss the unfortunate corpse into the air with sheer glee: all those years of having to behave nicely when she belonged to the old lady were behind her now, and she clearly relished the opportunities I gave her to run her paws through the grass, and pounce about in the shrubs.

More than once, I tried to explain to her that killing immobile animals didn't really constitute a challenging hunt, but Muffin could not have cared less. Grimly – for the deed, being done, was out of my hands – I allowed Muff her victory laps in the courtyard. She'd toss the tiny critters into the air and roll around with them on the grass before I gingerly disposed of them, and offered a small apology to the Gods for their untimely demise. Clearly, it was not a matter of Muffin not liking to hunt; it was a matter of Muffin wanting the hunt to be *easy*.

Buddy and Spanky had no such qualms when it came to the challenges of rodent hunting. They displayed an extraordinary amount of patience waiting, as they did, for weeks on end for an opportunity to present itself. Naturally, one finally did.

I was lying in bed reading, late one night, when an excited passel of cats raced into the room and swarmed

around the bedside table. The small grey mouse cow-
ered under the nightstand while I held the cats at bay.
They weren't intent on killing their prey, at this point;
mostly, they were keen to get a look at the tiny interloper
whom, Buddy and Spanky, at least, had never seen the
like of before. Mindful that the mouse was already in
defensive mode, I took care to avoid putting my hands
within biting range as I shooed the little fellow into my
bathroom wastebasket.

My mind raced as I wondered what to do with him
next: it was the middle of winter, and frightfully cold
out. I could not, in good conscience, send him outside
when he didn't have a warm home waiting for him. His
warm home was *my* warm home, after all, and the cats',
as well, so there was no way I could let him go inside the
house, either. An interim solution was the only answer.

As I was not inclined to get dressed and go out into
the night to find a store to deal with questions of mouse
habitat, I simply emptied out a clear plastic storage container that had been keeping my summer clothes tidy
until spring, and installed the mouse within. I supplied
him with a small dish of water, a handful of sunflower
seeds, and some shredded material of the sort one uses
when mailing something fragile. This would have to suf-
fice until morning, and with that thought, I sealed the
lid on the container and bid the cats goodnight.

It was Spanky for whom the new visitor held the most
interest. He never ventured far from the container, and
when he saw the mouse moving about within, he would
leap at it, clearly puzzled as to what this structure was
which prevented his access. He frequently asked me
when he would be allowed to eat the mouse, though it

must be noted that Spanky didn't mean this in the literal sense; he seemed to confuse "eat" and "play" – both in word and concept, though perhaps the fault is mine for not possessing the feline language equivalent of "playing with prey before you kill it."

In any case, the next morning I went to the store and purchased a mouse cage and immediately regretted it. It was much too small, and the thought occurred to me that if I were a mouse in captivity, I would want plenty of elbow room. I went back to the store and bought a storage container identical to the one he had spent the night in: now I had a container for my clothes, *and* one for the mouse.

My next task was to walk from my home to the park across the street to gather supplies. By the end of my walk, I had collected a handsome number of mouse necessities: twigs, dried leaves, curled strips of bark, pine needles. I spent a ridiculous amount of time arranging them *just so* in the storage container, trying for a sort of recognizable mouse ambiance; I wanted him to feel at home. And, with cat faces leering at him through the clear plastic, I wanted him to feel safe.

He made the most of his new surroundings. He hid in the curled strips of bark, and foraged among the leaves and twigs for the sunflower seeds I set out in strategic places. I wanted him to have to hunt for his food, as my intention was to house him through the rest of the winter, then release him outside in spring. I already had a suitable release site in mind.

In the meantime, he had an eye injury that I suspected the cats of inflicting. One eye bulged rather precariously, and it was unclear whether he could even see with it. I consulted Dr. Jill, and was advised to wait and see what happened. His health appeared otherwise good, so I left him to deal with his eye as he saw fit. Thankfully, in time, the swelling subsided and his appearance returned to normal.

I elected to give the little fellow a simple name that the cats would understand, though in retrospect, I probably could have made a wiser choice. In the interest of clarity, I referred to every individual cat toy as a "mice." No matter what it looked like, if it was a cat toy, it was called *mice*. And so was our new resident.

I didn't realize at the time that I was fomenting a certain amount of confusion among the cats. On the one hand, I was telling them that they couldn't eat our new friend, and on the other hand, I was referring to that new friend as one of their toys. This may explain the look of puzzlement that remained on Spanky's face for over a month.

I came to enjoy Mice as much for his indomitable spirit as for the entertainment he provided the cats. I admired his determination to tell me what-for, like the times when I would offer him my finger to smell and instead of sniffing, he would rear up on his hind legs and give that finger a mighty shove with his front feet. His message was clear: *We will not be developing a friendship.*

The container remained in my bedroom, where an afternoon sunbeam provided Mice with additional ambience and Vitamin D. Once a week, I fished him out and put him in the original, too-small container so that I could clean the larger home. The twigs, bark, and leaves would be replaced, and a new arrangement created for him to puzzle over. Spanky was always very enthusiastic about 'helping,' and tried more than once to climb into the container.

About a month and a half after his arrival, I noticed that Mice had created a project for himself - he was slowly but surely chewing his way to freedom. I understood: his eye had healed; it was time to go. It took him several days' work to chew a hole big enough to crawl out of, and I let him do it. If he waited out the winter, I would have released him in spring, but this was the choice he made (New Hampshire's state motto is *Live Free or Die*, which gives one pause for thought) and I felt compelled to respect it.

He disappeared without a trace, and life resumed its usual tempo until, about a week later, I awoke one morning to find a mouse corpse lying on the bedroom floor. Saddened, and more than a little disgusted with my feline friends – who all received an "I am *not* amused" lecture – I made the necessary preparations. On a scrap of tissue, I wrote a brief prayer, "Please bless this mouse and give him a good home with you." I wrapped Mice in the tissue and placed him in a small cardboard box.

Owing to a brief thaw in an otherwise wintry February, I was just able to dig a hole large enough to accommodate Mice's coffin. He would not be the last mouse to meet an untimely demise at the chicken coop, but he would be the one I held in highest esteem. And, as a mark of respect for the lesson he taught me, all future surviving mice were immediately released outside, where they could live free.

My mother turned a blind eye to the abuse. If you pretend that nothing is happening, then you don't have to deal with it. The cost of that willful ignorance to my mother's soul has yet to be assessed. The cost to me has been a lifetime of damage control: bankruptcy, a stint in a psych ward, depression, Post Traumatic Stress Disorder, multiple suicide attempts, too many therapists to count. Years lost that I can never have again.

The struggle for meaning, and against bitterness, is an endless one. There are days when depression wins, and days when the quack of a happy duck trumps all, and I have no control whatsoever as to which one of those days it will be.

The Gang

(Part Three)

There were two big events at McKinnon's Pond, the following summer. The first involved the arrival of two more large white ducks – dumped, like the others, by thoughtless humans. They initially had no interest in the pond itself, and instead spent their first day huddled together near the boathouse. Sam advised me to let them acclimate in their own good time and, indeed, the very next day found them paddling happily alongside the others in the water.

Owing to their outgoing and assertive natures, I promptly dubbed the new arrivals Frick and Frack. They were far more accustomed to humans than Sid and Sol, the two original white fellows, and quickly established themselves as the greediest ducks on the pond by shouldering their way to the head of the hand-out line.

They weren't bullies; they were simply very single-minded in their pursuit of food.

From Frick and Frack I learned that there are three small, sharp, hook-shaped appendages protruding from the end of a duck's webbed feet. I presume that they use these appendages to scratch for food at the bottom of the pond, though I only learned of their existence when Frick (or Frack – who could tell the difference?) used them for another purpose: to secure his perch on my naked leg.

It was part of their charm that the new ducks felt comfortable enough in our relationship to climb onto my lap to get a better angle on the bag of corn. They thought nothing of putting their bills right into the bag and helping themselves to the contents, and sometimes this involved perching on my crossed legs. I could tolerate the ensuing pain for only a few seconds before I found it necessary to pick up the offending duck and set him back on the ground. The new guys never seemed to mind being handled this way.

Frick and Frack made themselves at home quite quickly, and no one among the pond's residents seemed to object to the addition. Indeed, the five large ducks formed their own clique within the general group. Perhaps they'd been aware all along of the size and color differences between themselves and the wild mallards.

The size difference posed a number of questions in my mind when I became aware, that spring, that Missy Miss had acquired a beau, and that this new chap was a wild mallard – easily half her size. As I sat on the ground during a feed, I noticed Missy take a few steps away from the group and begin to preen her feathers. A small drake followed her and stood by, watching. After a few minutes, she moved a few more steps away and preened anew. The new chap moved with her this time, as well.

After watching this curious Missy-dance for a few days, I drew the obvious conclusion. She was clearly very pleased with the turn of events and indeed, when I remarked, "Missy Miss! You have a boyfriend!," she positively glowed. At some point, she disappeared onto her nest and only occasionally left it to feed with me.

I didn't hold out much hope for a successful union – I simply couldn't see how that poor fellow would surmount the size issue. My worry was that Missy would sit on a nest of useless eggs, not understanding that they weren't going to hatch. As it turned out, *I* was clearly the one who didn't understand: approaching the pond for a feed one day, I was pleased and surprised by the sight of Missy paddling toward me, trailed by eleven fuzzy ping pong balls.

Eleven! My word! I was accustomed to moms with six ducklings, or occasionally eight, but eleven was unprecedented on the pond. And, owing to the two different breeds, the babies came in a festive variety of colors: some were black, some were yellow; some were black *with* yellow; one or two had standard mallard markings; some had black splotches on otherwise orange feet. All of them possessed eager, adventurous personalities, as if they couldn't wait to get out and see the world.

It must be said that Miss was not a good mother. At the outset, I had optimistically hoped that seven of the eleven ducklings would survive to adulthood. It soon became clear that there was no way that many would live: between the hawks, the snapping turtles, the neighborhood cats, and Missy's cavalier approach to child-rearing, those ducklings were dropping like flies.

Virtually every time I arrived for a feed, instead of bringing the kids along, Miss simply abandoned her young in favor of a meal – leaving them, literally, as sitting ducks out on the pond. Lord knows what other parenting felonies she committed when I wasn't there. Ultimately, I would be left to vent to Sam, yet again, that, "Nature *sucks!*"

Two good things came out of Missy's bad mothering, though. First, because she was relatively fearless about approaching me for food, her children grew up to be unafraid of me, too. They teemed around me from a young age, making photo-ops of themselves almost very single day. Secondly, the babies' trust in me brought out some hidden reserve of courage in Miss that changed our relationship forever.

I was sitting cross-legged on the ground, tossing chunks of bread – Missy's favorite food. There were twenty-odd ducks milling about, along with the babies, who pecked and peeped and chased each other around. In the midst of all this activity, I felt a gentle tug on the back of my shirt. When I glanced over my shoulder, I found Missy Miss looking up at me expectantly, and the message was clear: "I want some, too!" It was an extraordinary moment.

While she seemed unconcerned about being in close proximity to me, Missy had studiously avoided touching me – and being touched – for over a year. Even my most gentle attempts at petting had resulted in her shying away with a speed I hadn't known she possessed. I'd no idea that she had been watching me with her children, all these weeks, and evidently reaching some duck conclusions about my trustworthiness.

Unfortunately, my trustworthiness couldn't protect the little nippers from the ravages of nature, and ultimately, only three of Missy's young would survive to adulthood. These three I named Pretty Lady, Big Boy, and Pretty Boy, who, with his all-black feathers and white breast, would stand out on the pond like a sore thumb for years to come.

Junebug

I have, among my acquaintances, a couple who enjoyed a relationship of long standing with a cat named Robert, pronounced in the French fashion with a silent 't'. When the elderly cat's kidneys began to fail, my friends did everything in their power to sustain his life and keep him comfortable, from special diets to subcutaneous infusions of saline solution.

Those sub-cu infusions – a tremendously intimate undertaking for veterinary amateurs – solidified the bonds of their relationship with Robert in a way that fourteen years of kibble and catnip never could, and when his time came to die, my friends were devastated. Cheating death, as they had for twenty-three months, tends to make you feel invincible, and in the wake of Robert's death, they floundered.

Life went on, as it must do, but Robert's passing left an enormous void; the silence was deafening and their home, suddenly much too big. In an effort to fill the gaping hole in their hearts, my friends acquired another cat. And another. And still another. At last count, they had eleven.

The fact that most of those cats remain strictly outdoors is neither here nor there. The fact that there are now eleven cats in the family is the point, and it's a problem I have struggled with myself: a large presence leaves large paws to fill, and one or two cats with small personalities simply doesn't cut it.

Which explains my acquisition of Buddy – who was standoffish as a kitten, and remains so to this day; Spanky – who desperately wanted a family of his own, but had spent too much time alone and frightened to allow me to get close; and, finally, Junebug – who, along with her own cheerful personality, seems to have gotten a nudge from my beloved Winkie, and fills the bill nicely. Throw in Muffin, who's been with me for ages, and you have enough cats for a rubber of Bridge.

I never intended to have four cats. Two seemed plenty and, indeed, when Winkie was alive, two *was* enough. When he passed, my poor torn heart ached from the loss of his presence. I resisted the temptation to run right out and adopt another cat, though. Instead, I waited until an opportunity presented itself, which it did several months later when Sam, who was no doubt trying to help me through my grief, put me in touch with a woman whose kittens needed homes. I can't say that Buddy charmed me especially, but he was a cute little fellow, and I had room for him in my heart and house.

Because his mother was feral, Buddy felt no particular inclination to develop a bond with me and, in fact, our relationship is more that of roommates than friends. The only way I know he feels any fondness at all is that when I go to bed at night, he's always the first one to join me, staking his claim to a spot next to my right calf. He doesn't like to be held, and he rarely tolerates petting. He's a loner who prefers the solitary comfort of his favorite spot in the linen cupboard. Which is why I felt no pangs of guilt when I considered adding Spanky to the family.

Spanky had been abandoned at the animal hospital as a kitten. Sam took him home with a view to adding him to her indoor menagerie (not to be confused with her outdoor menagerie, which is a separate entity and considerably larger), but he was so frightened by the dog, the kids, and the other cats, that he used a daughter's bed as his litter box. He was promptly relegated to the purgatory that is the rabbit cage (*sans* rabbit), where he would remain – alone and lonely – until he was big enough to join the barn cats. The daughter with the soiled bed linens named him 'Linus'.

"*Linus?!*" I sputtered in disbelief as I peered at him through the wire, "he's not a Linus! He's more of a Spanky." My friend said nothing – thinking, no doubt, that she had already hooked me, and now simply needed to reel me in. "He's a cute little guy," I remarked, to which Sam replied that he was one of the prettiest orange tabbies she'd ever seen. She was about to give me the grand tour of her property, so I pulled the wary kitty from his purgatory and tucked him inside my shirt; only his head peeped out at the collar.

We strolled the grounds, Sam pointing out the neighbor's pond where she and an offspring had rescued a group of motherless ducklings, and stopping to show me where Spotty – beloved horse of Jenna – was buried. Throughout our walk, Spanky remained inside my shirt, and seemed to enjoy the outing. Somewhere between the pond and the pet cemetery, I concluded that he should come home with me. I was not surprised that my friend agreed.

While it was obvious to me that Spanky wanted a family, it escaped me that he wanted a *cat* family: he took to Muffin like a fish to water, not asking, but *demanding* that she take notice and care for him. Which left plenty of room in that void in my heart. *Something* was missing – unbearably so – from my relationships with Buddy and Spanky, and it was this indefinable thing which left me feeling a little empty.

I taught both Buddy and Spanky to walk on a leash, and they did well after a fashion, although neither would ever attempt a walk to the duck pond. After I moved to the chicken coop, which is situated on an old estate, both cats readily took to walking the grounds, sniffing out exciting evidence of rabbits, deer, and woodchucks. But in a way, I was simply going through the motions of a dance that had lost its meaning the day Winkie died. Then I ran an errand to Dr. Green's office.

I always tried to time those visits to coincide with when Sam worked: I hardly ever got to see her otherwise. I would make my purchase and then chat for as long as time and other clients permitted. On this day, business was slow, and my friend directed me to open the communicating door to the kennels, where I was instructed to peek into the first cage on the right. Housed within were a mother cat and several young.

Sam was planning to take them all home and make them barn cats this very day: another batch of abandoned animals that Dr. Green's staff had lovingly cared for and assumed responsibility of. My friend came out from behind the counter and pulled a small grey tabby from the cage, remarking as she did that all the kittens had delightful personalities and, "Look at the pretty smile on this one!"

She does these things on purpose. She knows I'm fond of tabbies, and she knows I'm fond of smiling cats. It's entirely calculated, and I knew even as she spoke that I was being ruthlessly manipulated, but I looked at the smiling kitty anyway and groaned, "Oh, all *right!*" Sam arranged a container for the kitten to travel in safely, and threw in some cat food to boot, all in less time than it takes to sneeze, hoping, I'm sure, to send me on my way before I had a chance to stop and think about the small grey tabby who was now looking up at me trustingly from inside the box. By the time I got her home, I had named her Junebug.

They all hated her on sight – especially Muffin, who had had enough of raising other people's kittens. All three cats went on strike, growling and hissing in protest for weeks on end and scaring hell out of Junebug in the process. Buddy's contribution to the general mayhem came in the form of his attempts to escape.

Evidently concluding that four cats were at least one too many, he hatched a plan that went undetected until the day I noticed that the curtain which covers the large pane of glass in my front door had begun to look inexplicably frayed. This puzzled me – it's not as if that piece of fabric ever *does* anything that would cause it to show wear – until a closer examination revealed a number of holes the size of claws.

The mystery was solved the day I walked into the hallway and found Buddy climbing the curtain. Mind you, he wasn't just climbing, he was trying to decipher how the doorknob worked. How many times had he seen my hand do *something* in the vicinity of that knob which resulted in an open door? And now he was determined to figure it out for himself.

I told him repeatedly that I didn't want him to go, that I'd be lonely without him, but he dismissed my words with a sullen, "I'm *goin'*, Kelly," every time. After several weeks of failed attempts, though, he appeared to resign himself to the inevitability of spending the rest of his life with us, and stopped climbing the curtain.

Frightened by the nasty reception she received, Junebug came running to me, and I became Momma. It was an arrangement that suited and amused me: if I stayed too long in the shower, she would take up a position on the other side of the curtain and squeak her fear of being left alone out there with the bullies. She followed me all over the house, and purred happily whenever I scooped her onto my lap. Junebug ultimately endeared herself to me the day she gave me a Winkie-style wake-up call.

Winkie had developed a tried-and-true wake-up method. He would sit on my pillow and gently nibble my ear – being careful not to break the skin or cause me pain. When the nibbles failed to rouse me (which they invariably did: I loved this routine so much that I always feigned sleep in the hopes that he would keep at it), he would step up his efforts. Putting both front paws on my head, he would knead my scalp, purring ferociously as he gave me a massage I couldn't help but notice, with just enough claw action to get my attention without hurting me. It was a carefully choreographed dance, one I treasured deeply during our time together, and missed dreadfully after his death.

When I awoke one morning to find Junebug tattooing the same dance on my scalp, I lay there listening to her purr, and thinking, "I know you're here, Winkie!" *Always with you, Kelly!* echoed in my head as I realized that Winkie had finally found a successor he could work with. Not to make into an exact replica of him, but to teach: *do this, it's what Kelly needs.*

Junebug appears to be an apt student: while she's never done the Winkie Wake-Up Dance again, she's displayed an unstinting cheerfulness and loyalty. She alone chooses to sleep next to my pillow at night, and she alone approaches me with toys in her mouth, asking me to play.

She is manifestly *not* Winkie. Apart from anything else, she has tortoiseshell in her genes, giving her a distinctly un-Winkie-like stubborn streak. Many's the time I've issued a sharp "No!", only to watch her continue the offending behavior *on purpose.* When I tell her that I don't actually like claws digging into my skin, she protests, "But *I* like claws, Kelly!" Where my other three cats readily acquiesce, Junebug seems determined to dig in her heels and have her own way as a matter of principal. It's annoying, and it's amusing, and I can only hope that she'll listen to me when it really matters.

I've read with interest the news reports regarding pet cloning. Apparently, a U.S. concern is already open for business, ready to turn Fluffy's DNA into Fluffy II. I admit I was prepared to consider the possibilities – until a scientist cautioned that while they are able to replicate DNA, they *cannot* replicate an individual's unique personality.

There was a time when Winkie needed daily medication, and I tried to soften the unpleasantness of shoving pills down his throat by rewarding him with a dish of wet food, after. Of course, it would have been cruel not to include Muffin – who loves wet food – so our morning ritual became pill, syringe full of liquid medicine, then the reward. As I stood portioning the stuff, I provided the same commentary every single day, "Some for Muffin, and some for Winkie," to which Winkie *always*, without fail, replied cheekily, "*More for me, Kelly!*"

As deeply felt as the loss of Winkie continues to be, I cannot imagine going to the trouble and expense of creating an identical copy, only to be disappointed that it never utters those much-loved words, "*More for me, Kelly!*" Better, I think, to grieve the loss and then move on to the next unique personality, like a torti-tabby who declares, "But I *like* to claw!"

Author's Note:

Some time after this story was written, the daughter with the soiled bed linens – A.K.A. "Alyssa" – revealed that she had been angry with me for taking Linus/Spanky, because she considered him hers. It was a reasonable consideration given that my friend had brought him home from Dr. Green's office on Alyssa's birthday.

"But she *told* me to take him," I spluttered defensively and, waving my hand in the general direction of the offending hutch, continued, "she sent him to the *rabbit cage!*" "I know," Alyssa replied, "I was mad about that, too."

While I'm not inclined to return Spanky to Alyssa – he's been an integral member of Team Meister for a number of years now, after all – I *did* promise, in an effort to assuage hurt feelings, to mention the dear girl's name – which is Alyssa – in this book.

He's Not Even My Horse

His name is Obie, and although my friend Sam and her husband Farrell pay for the feed and the farrier, there is no doubt in anyone's mind that the Appaloosa belongs to their daughter, Red. She trained on him, they competed, they have a Thing.

I saw this Thing in action at my friend's annual bonfire. Each October, she and Farrell invite everyone over for a barbecue, the highlight of which is the ignition of a years'-worth of stuff that's been relegated to the pile for just this purpose. Over the course of many months, folks 'donate' all sorts of items: sofas, old lumber, things they're eager to unload but can't, anywhere else. On the designated night, after sunset, Farrell torches the lot of it as people stand around, mildly drunk, munching on bratwurst. The blaze never fails to impress.

One year, when the wind was dangerously high, Farrell flatly refused to light the fire. Pressure from Sam found her husband reluctantly agreeing to go ahead with the planned fireworks display. The man in charge of setting them off began lighting fuses, and a modest but eye-catching show ensued directly over the paddock – which Obie was standing in at the time.

Red saw the problem before anyone else did, and began hollering for Dad to make the fireworks guy stop until she could stable her horse. Because of a communications glitch between the two men, though, the fireworks continued, with bright colors exploding into noisy bangs. Red ran right into the paddock, seized Obie's halter, and, hanging on tight, simply stood and waited. To do anything else would have increased Obie's panic and created an even more dangerous situation.

Red had shooed me out of the paddock for my safety, but she clearly didn't seem at all concerned with her own: *Obie* was her one and only priority. As the two of them stood beneath the shower of pyrotechnics, it became clear to me what an awesome thing trust is, for there was Red – all five foot nothin', ninety-eight pounds of her – standing in front of a frightened thousand-pound animal, telling him soothingly, "It's o.k., Obie, you're o.k." And here's the Thing: Obie stood there *believing her.*

He could have mashed Red into the ground with one hoof, had he chosen to, but Obie had clearly invested enough trust in his mistress to figure, if she's going to stand here and insist that things are fine, the least I can do is try to believe her. From my vantage point on the other side of the fence I watched them, fascinated. Funny thing is, once Red got him stabled, Obie stuck his head out the window and watched the remaining fireworks along with everyone else.

My friend Sam is one of those rare beings who insist that you come to visit whenever *you* want to. It doesn't matter a jot to her whether she is home to receive you or not, and she backs up this claim by showing you where, on the property, the spare key to the back door is hidden. While I prefer to visit when I know my friend is home, I *have* availed myself of her invitation, even when I knew in advance that no one would be there. The reason was Obie.

I came to horses in my early forties. After a failed bid with ice-skating lessons that resulted in a fractured skull, I decided to try riding lessons; I'd always loved horses, and I wasn't getting any younger. But the lessons – one hour each, twice a month, involved a fairly brief amount of time in the horse's company. It was a start, but not nearly enough. My friend's open-door policy gave me all the horse hours I wanted.

Obie wasn't particularly rideable anymore – advancing age, combined with serious foot problems, kept even Red on the ground most of the time. I wasn't really looking to ride him, anyway. Mostly, it was enough to simply commune with him, to groom and contemplate life with him while he stood, patiently munching on the treats I invariably brought him. "Buy one, get one free" sales on bags of carrots always guaranteed a visit, and Obie came to recognize me as That Person Who Gives Me Snacks. I dubbed my time with him Horse Therapy, a time to clear my mind as I attended to this gentle giant.

"You're not gonna rat me out to the redhead, are you," I inquired anxiously of my friend. It became something of a familiar refrain as Obie's foot problems continued to flare and wane. The farrier had even put him on a special diet – if for no other reason than because less weight meant less strain on already stressed feet. Obie was, by then, the equine version of a couch potato, and had gotten noticeably chunkier. The diet, therefore, was a good idea, but it threw a bit of a wrench into my attempts to spoil him.

Red took these things very seriously – more so even than the mom who paid the farrier bills, and she issued the admonition that perhaps the treats should wait awhile. Unbeknownst to Red, though, virtually *everyone* was giving Obie treats when she wasn't looking, and Sam's response to my repeated inquiries became, "I won't tell on you if you don't tell on me." Partners in crime! Somehow, Obie managed to lose weight in spite of us.

He had had a buddy in the paddock, an attitudinal Haflinger by the name of Bippy. Bippy belonged to someone else but lived with Obie so that they could keep each other company. Being herd animals, horses prefer the fellowship of other horses, and depression in isolated animals is not uncommon.

When Bippy's owner decided to sell him, I worried about Obie's well-being. There was vague talk of getting some fainting goats, at one time, and vague talk of acquiring a miniature horse, another time, but nothing ever came of it and eventually, my frustration overcame my sense of *it's none of your business*: I sat down and composed a letter to the family. From Obie.

In it, Obie reminded them how hard he had worked, over the years, and how much he loved his human family.

The letter went on to tell them how lonely he was, and that he wondered what he had done wrong to end up in such a purgatory. I freely admit it: I heaped on the guilt. Then I signed off, "Love, Obie," put a stamp on the envelope, and mailed the thing.

What response the letter drew at its destination I cannot say, for my friend has never volunteered an opinion on the subject, but she's still talking to me, which is a good sign. Obie, alas, is still alone, but admittedly, he doesn't seem to suffer for it. A country-western radio station plays continuously in the barn, and Obie appears to be every bit as patient with his lot in life as those around him who put up with me.

There was appalling insanity. Years of it. Alcoholism, suicide attempts, endless depression, rage at the world. I spent seven years living with a crack addict, trying to save him. It was, of course, me who needed saving, but it would be over two decades before I came to my rescue.

I owned a cat in those days. I wasn't a very good friend to her. Numb and detached, it never occurred to me that she might've needed more than just food, water, and the occasional scraps of attention I gave her. I didn't take good care of myself in those years. To this day, I feel a pang of sadness that I didn't take good care of her, either.

The Gang

(PART FOUR)

After three summers, I came to see that life on the pond mirrored life in general – which may seem patently obvious to the reader, but was in no way so to me, until I had experienced several seasons of life and death, struggle and survival. I suppose I'd assumed that my small haven would somehow be exempt from life's trials; after all, why *should* such benign creatures be made to suffer nature's cruel vagaries? But this, as my friend Sam so patiently explained, was life, was *nature,* was the cycle of things.

Missy Miss disappeared, that spring. Considering the fact that in our three-year relationship I had never once seen this domestic duck fly, it was a puzzling turn of events. Frick and Frack – the late arrivals, vanished around the same time, and the disappearance of all three remains a mystery to this day, though it's safe to assume that predators were involved.

When I realized that my feedings had been three large ducks short for over a week, I reached out to pet one of the remaining white fellows, to see who had been left behind. At the touch of my hand, he skittered away – as did the other white duck at a later attempt – which told me that my original shy guys, Sid and Sol, remained.

Since the ducks belonged to no one in particular, and since the City had thus far taken a hands-off approach to things fowl, there was no one I could ask about Missy, although, for lack of any better ideas, I *did* leave a message with the Animal Control Officer, asking if the City had suddenly decided to remove ducks from the pond. I received a rather vague reply, informing me that the City had taken no action and that perhaps the ducks had simply decided to fly away. It seemed a bit too easy.

A month or so after Missy disappeared, her daughter, Pretty Lady, produced six ducklings. Lady had grown to be as large as her mother and, like Miss, had acquired a standard mallard beau. Lady had been a bit more discreet about her courtship than Missy, though, so her offspring came as somewhat of a surprise. And, like Lady's own siblings, the new ducklings came in a festive variety of colors. The only real difference between Missy's brood and Lady's – and it was striking – was the style of parenting.

Lady had obviously learned from her mother's mistakes: she kept her offspring well away from everything even remotely threatening, including me. For some weeks, Lady maintained a distance from me at the feedings, preferring to peck around the edges of the group for stray corn. If a baby became frightened and peeped, she immediately gathered them all up and left. Initially, I was saddened by Lady's behavior, but it didn't take long for me to get over it and champion her instincts. At some point I realized that this was the ducklings' best hope for survival, and it was actually quite refreshing to see a good mother among the ducks.

When the young ones were over a month old, Lady finally allowed them to get near me during a feed. By this time, they had developed a natural caution about their surroundings – and the hulking giant sitting among them. As long as I observed the rules on noise and movement, they remained calm enough. Perhaps because of their reserve, I never felt inclined to name them; to this day, I refer to each of them simply as "Baby."

Of the original six ducklings, three survived. It wasn't a bad average, all things considered. Big Boy and Pretty Boy seemed content to play Uncle, and the little ones appeared to recognize the big ducks as family. All of the domestic ducks continued to band together, slowly increasing their modest flock, and none among them seemed troubled by the new additions. Lady's beau disappeared altogether, making him, in my view, a cad among ducks.

I came to be aware, that summer, of a number of fishing line injuries among the ducks. The City stocked the pond with a variety of fish – although you were expected to throw most of them back – and children, in particular, were encouraged to fish as they pleased.

I have every reason to believe that it was those careless young clots who caused the injuries, by thoughtlessly leaving lengths of fishing line lying around for duck legs to get wound up in. It often wrapped so tightly as to cut into the flesh of the leg, causing the afflicted duck to limp, at best, and be attacked as an unwelcome weakling by the other ducks, at worst.

Matters came to a head when I noticed the drake with the pronounced limp. Day by day, the injury worsened until, in desperation, I bought a long-handled fishing net, in the hopes of capturing the unfortunate fellow. The local paper had recently announced the addition of an Avian Specialist at one of the veterinary clinics. But the drake was, alas, a wild animal, and never allowed himself to get within grabbing range. Helplessly, I watched as, over a period of two weeks, his right leg rotted away and finally, literally, *fell off.* It was heartbreaking. All that remained was half a leg – a stump – and how would he manage over winter? How would he feed, and mate, and migrate?

Well, the little duck was nothing if not plucky, which is exactly what I named him. Trying to make his recovery easier, I took to tossing corn at waters' edge, so that he could eat without having to hop about on land. Gaily, I would call out, *"Where's Plucky?"* attempting to ascertain where, precisely, I should throw the corn. He learned his name so quickly that I soon noticed one mallard – who looked exactly like every other mallard, but for the stump where his leg used to be – bobbing his head above the crowd as if to say, "I'm here!"

When the others tried to nip at him and send him away, Plucky nipped right back and sent *them* scurrying! He survived by sheer grit and determination and by golly!, if he wasn't up and peg-legging around on dry land by fall! I don't remember ever being filled with as much respect and admiration as I was for Plucky. It was as if he considered the loss of a leg a minor impediment, and simply got on with it.

A few weeks after Plucky lost his leg, and still shaken by my utter helplessness in the matter, I watched as a small female limped up to a morning feed. She was easily within grabbing range, and that fishing line trailing behind her needed removed before it did Plucky-type damage. I decided that when things settled down in a few minutes, I would grab her up and take her to this Avian Specialist. But of course, by the time *I* thought the time was right, she had limped out of range. I spent the rest of the day being very annoyed with myself, and saying prayers to the Gods to give me another chance the next morning. Apparently, they were listening.

I sat down on the ground the following day and calmly scattered corn. She came limping up the bank and settled in a foot or so away from me. Casually, I gathered up the bags of corn, scooped her into my arms, and headed for the car. She made a few initial squeaks of protest and then remained quiet for the duration of the adventure.

I had put one of my cat carriers in the car for just this purpose, and I deposited her into it now. She rode in the passenger seat and eyed me curiously as I drove to the clinic, explaining along the way that we would be visiting a nice lady doctor who would tend to her leg. The duck seemed to take this news in stride, and offered up no comment.

When we arrived, I was told that the Avian Specialist wasn't due in until the afternoon and anyway, they weren't, by law, licensed to work on wild animals. As I digested this, the doctor whose practice it was joined in the discussion. I explained to him the simple nature of the duck's problem, and with a nudge and a wink, it was suggested that I take her into the exam room.

A staffer held the duck carefully while Doctor went to work. The fishing line was more deeply imbedded than he had initially thought, and it took some diligence to remove it. All the while, the duck made no noise, and betrayed no distress, although curiously, her eyes remained trained on me throughout the ordeal. I stood on the opposite side of the exam table, staring right back and whispering gentle words of reassurance.

When Doctor finished with her leg, he decided that a shot of steroid, and another of antibiotic, would be in order. Not being an avian specialist, he had no idea of the correct dosages and spent some minutes consulting various books on the subject. As he gave her the injections, both he and his staffer remarked on how well-behaved she'd been. Indeed, I, myself, was impressed: for a wild animal who had never in her life ridden in a car, been inside a building of any kind, or been handled by humans, she had remained steadfastly courageous, and I said as much to her on the drive back to the pond.

As I was loading her into the carrier for that trip, Doctor surprised me by saying that there was no charge for his services – services that I had walked into his clinic quite prepared to pay. He said that he would be writing off the expense as research. He made the small request that I return in a weeks' time and give him, for his records, an update on the duck. I was more than happy to agree to, and comply with, his request.

Once back at the pond, I removed the carrier from the car and strode toward the water. I noticed that the duck was turned wrong-way-round inside, with her rear end facing the carrier door. A breeze came off the water, greeting us with familiar pond smells. The little duck got one whiff and in a trice, she had righted herself, pecking now at the bars of the carrier door and making small excited squeaky noises. I set the carrier down, opened the door and stood watching as she raced into the water.

I saw her a few times after that – enough times to be able to tell Doctor that I'd seen improvement in her, and then she melded into the duck crowd and disappeared. Whether she flew away, or remained on the pond, I couldn't say, but that's a good thing: she's obviously not limping anymore, if I can't spot her.

While I'm quietly satisfied with my role in this rescue, it must be said that I wouldn't recommend this sort of thing to others: they are wild animals, and we have intruded upon them enough without dragging them off to vile-smelling buildings peopled with, well.... *people*, and putting them through unaccustomed procedures. Better, I think, to teach our careless young clots to stop being so careless.

Tommy

The circumstances of life at the chicken coop are thus: less than forty feet to the right of my home is what I believe used to be the caretaker's house. It is the only purpose-built house on the property. My landlord rents this house to a fifty-ish couple, Jack and Sharon. My landlord, his wife, and their children reside in what was once a cow barn. Cleverly converted, it is a large airy space with a central rectangular column made from local field stones, comprising the staircase to the upper floor on one side, and a substantial fireplace on the other. This former barn sits less than thirty feet to the left of the chicken coop. It goes without saying that quarters are very close indeed.

I would like to say that we all get along marvelously, and on the surface, we do pretty well. But beneath the pretense lies the fact that my landlord and his wife are the most self-absorbed people I've ever met. Nowhere is this more obvious to me than in the cavalier way they treat the tabby cat and two dogs who are their pets.

The dogs – secure behind an electronic fence which gives them the run of the property – are so hopelessly stupid that I've caught them trying to eat all manner of things, up to and including *glass.* Huey and Dewey weren't born stupid; the fault lies entirely with Lord and Lady Witless, who grin as they tell you that the dogs "flunked" obedience school.

Lord and Lady seem to believe that the dogs have no practical needs to contend with. Discipline, supervision, interaction: these are things that involve an ongoing commitment of time and energy, two things the Witlesses clearly don't wish to be bothered with. It was bad enough to watch the dogs wandering mindlessly about the property day after week after month, searching for *something* with which to occupy themselves, and generally finding it in the dumpster. But when I realized that they were being left outside for hours at a stretch with *no food or water,* I lost a large measure of respect for the Witlesses.

The problem is, I *like* my chicken coop home. To say something directly would have guaranteed my receiving an invitation to leave. And to report these two careless people to the authorities would have brought the same results. I toyed briefly with the idea of dognapping, and having them euthanized, but this seemed unfair, and more than a little presumptuous. Instead, I ground my teeth and headed to my local Target.

There, I selected a medium-sized plastic storage container. It cost three dollars or so – not much, really, but it would serve the purpose nicely. Back at home, I chose

an out-of-the-way spot near the water spigot and proceeded to fill the cheap container full of water.

It didn't take long for the dogs to figure out that a
consistent source of fresh water was now available for
them, and they have relied on that cheap water dish now
for several summers. Huey and Dewey don't even bother
to look at the dismal offering from Lord and Lady: the
much-too-small metal bowl that they finally set out is
usually either mostly empty, blocked by a child's bicycle,
or full of dirt, twigs, and leaves. It is, frankly, a wonder
that the dogs survive at all.

Conversely, Larry the cat seems reasonably intelli-
gent, and in possession of enough in the way of survival
skills to keep himself alive when the Witlesses become
too preoccupied with their own lives to give him anything more than a passing thought. At eighteen pounds,
he's a big chunk of cat, with a brutal streak that's made
him locally famous for eviscerating an untold number
of woodland creatures.

Life at the coop involves nightly cat patrols during
which, as I lie in bed, Larry can be heard yowling as he
passes under my window. I've narrowed his pronounce-
ments to two possibilities: either he's informing us that
all is well, or he's announcing his intention to add four
cats to his list of victims.

One summer day, Lady Witless came knocking on
my door, wanting to know if I would be willing to feed
Larry while the family was away. She hadn't seen him
lately, though – would I keep an eye out for him? With
that, she was gone, and it fell to neighbor Sharon to tell
me what Lady clearly didn't know: that Larry was prone
to extended holidays, disappearing to who-knew-where

for several days at a time. I digested this news as I went about my day, a dish of dry cat food at the ready in case I heard that familiar yowling.

That familiar yowling came around midnight. I jumped out of bed, grabbed the dish and stood in the forecourt calling my customary, "Larry *cat!*" But it wasn't Larry who had yowled, and it wasn't Larry who appeared; it was a large tabby I had never seen before.

He looked to be about two years old and in good health, although he wasn't neutered, which is unusual in this day and age. He was initially wary, but the sight of food and a friendly face dropped his guard and he came forward eagerly, first head-butting my hand in thanks, then tucking into the food. He was very hungry indeed.

He came back a few more times, generally only at night, and always with a hearty appetite. After our initial meeting, he turned out to be quite social and friendly, but there was no way I could possibly take him in. The arrival of Junebug had utterly shattered Spanky's confidence and sense of purpose. His role as cute baby of the family had been poached by the new kitty, and, lacking any other obvious role to assume, Spanky floundered.

It concerned me to see the depth of sadness and confusion in his big green eyes, and it took all of my creative efforts to try to assuage some of that uncertainty. "But *you're* my favoritest cat of all, Spanky," I'd reassure him, "you're the bestest, specialest cat in the whole world!" This went on for well over a year before the veil of doubt began to lift, however slightly. To bring in yet another cat would destroy Spanky completely, and it was for this reason that I determined to catch the stray, have him neutered, then turn him into another of Sam's barn cats.

The only glitch in my plan was the fact that Sam had promised Farrell *no more cats*. I called a local rescue group about taking the stray, but they had no room for him. The best the woman could offer was to arrange to have the cat neutered at no cost to me. Conveniently, her organization worked with my vet, and Sam's boss, Dr. Green. When I dropped off the stray – "His name is *Tommy*," I announced – he charmed all and sundry (and, notably and especially, my friend) by being engaging and inquisitive. I gave him a hug and asked Sam to give him an extra helping of food; he still seemed hungry.

My friend's change of heart – and policy – occurred sometime between when I dropped Tommy off at Dr. Green's, and when I picked him up. As I stood chatting, the next day, telling her that I'd been unable to find a home for Tommy, she responded by saying, rather too loudly, "I'm sure the Humane Society will take good care of him." Pause. Wink. *Don't tell Debbie,* she mouthed. Debbie was the co-worker with the big yap. And then, in case I'd missed the point, "That's probably the best thing for him, the Humane Society." Pause. *Big* wink. *What I don't know, I can't get into trouble with my husband for,* she said under her breath. And then I understood: take Tommy out to the barn but don't tell her about it, which is, of course, exactly what I did.

I'd fallen into the habit of taking photos of the various critters I encountered, and the pictures from this adventure show Tommy poking his head out the carrier door, having a look around. I had set the carrier on the ground, just outside the barn, and the official greeter-cat, Bocephus, is in the photo, approaching Tommy in a friendly way. In fact, it was Bocephus who tried to give

Tommy a tour of the place, but Tommy was rattled by the turn of events: he'd laid quietly in the carrier during the drive to Sam's house because he had assumed that he was going home with me. Unfortunately, I was unaware of his assumption, and would remain so, until too late.

I'm embarrassed to admit, it never occurred to me to explain my plan to him. You'd think I would have learned that lesson when I was dealing with the injured raccoon, but apparently, even animal lovers can have moments of abject stupidity. To this day, I'm haunted by a nagging sense of guilt over the fact that I didn't understand until too late that *Tommy's* plan and *my* plan were entirely different. He disappeared, you see.

Sam assured me that this was normal. I had phrased the question as a hypothetical, a sort of, "If someone dropped off a cat somewhere, and then went to visit him but couldn't find him, what do you suppose?" She smiled knowingly as she told me that typically, new cats will hide for a couple of weeks, coming out at night to eat then going back into hiding while they adjust to their new surroundings. Eventually, they come out and take their place among the other cats. My friend had years of experience with this sort of thing, and her words were meant to reassure, but uncertainty gnawed at me.

Three weeks after I had dropped him off, Sam called late one night and left a message saying she had just spent twenty minutes in the barn petting Tommy. Thank goodness! I phoned her the next day, remarking on his consistency in making nocturnal visits. We arranged to go for a bite at our usual restaurant, and then stop at her place to see if we could coax him out again. At near to midnight, I stood outside the barn petting a cat whom I was fairly certain was not Tommy, while my friend insisted that he was. I took a few pictures of him, then sent the film off to be developed. The official verdict: *not* Tommy.

I showed Sam the two sets of photos, which she studied, agreeing that there were indeed two different cats involved. Then she looked up at me sharply and asked, "Well, then who the hell is *this*?" I had no answer, though my friend surmised that enough people knew of her barn cats that someone must have dropped off this one (now named "Timmy," though I wasn't even convinced that he was male), hoping that Sam would give him a good home.

We looked at each other in consternation, each for her own reasons: my friend, because she didn't want this animal-dumping thing to become a habit (and how could she stop it if she didn't know who was doing the dumping?), and myself because it was then that I realized the disparity in Tommy's and my plans. I felt *awful*. I had fully intended for him to have a pleasant barn cat life: other cats for companionship, huge bowls of kibble, mice to chase in neighboring cornfields, humans to fuss over him. It seemed idyllic.

But Tommy had wanted a home with me and, not knowing that, I had left him to his own devices at the barn. For months after, I added him to my nightly prayers, asking the Gods to look after Tommy wherever he was, and promising that if he turned up, I *would* take him home and make a place for him, regardless of how the other cats would feel about it. But it was a deal that the Gods apparently refused, for I have never seen Tommy again.

Meanwhile, the trend continues: three more cats have appeared at the barn under mysterious circumstances, a fact which puzzles my friend but frankly amuses me. Clearly, the word is out about the exceptional hospitality at the barn – a fact that Bocephus will gladly attest to.

Critterspeak

When I was younger – and far more reckless than I am now – I aspired to being a police officer. I even went so far as to take the Civil Service Test, a requirement for any civil servant, and a general indication of whether you possess working brain cells. One area of the test specifically intended for future law enforcement officers had to do with powers of observation.

You were instructed to study the picture on one page for a length of time, then move on to another page and record your observations without further recourse to the original page. I failed this portion of the test miserably. I was too busy memorizing the details of the outfit the man in the picture was wearing to notice that the woman on the other side of the street had both a gun *and* a canary in her hand.

There are still plenty of times when I'm a bit too distracted to take notice of my surroundings, but for the most part, I'm pleased to report that not only have I learned to stop and smell the roses, but I've learned to open my eyes and really *look* at the world. I've also developed the habit of sweeping my eyes from one side of the road to the other – wherever I am – checking to see if there are any animals in need of assistance.

It was with just this mindset that I strolled up the road to the park which lay across the street from my chicken coop home. Located in a quasi-rural setting, there are no sidewalks in the vicinity, which leaves me with two options: I can get in my car and drive the half-mile to the main entrance of the park – all the while wasting valuable fuel for no other reason than to get out of the car and *walk*, or I can hike the quarter-mile to the side entrance. This involves traveling along a grass verge, enduring occasional honks from passing motorists who seem to think that women will respond favorably to that sort of thing. I always choose the latterly approach and I was walking along the verge one fine evening when I noticed a robin, beak-down at the side of the road.

I'm not actually a fan of birds; they're too sharp and angular for my liking. I much prefer something soft and fuzzy that I can cuddle up with. But with the exception of spiders, I don't, as a rule, harbor ill will toward any animal – not even the big fat honking geese who are always so unkind to my gang of ducks during winter feeds. And there was something about that poor robin's pathetic ass-over-elbows posture which bothered me – bothered me to the point that, having passed the thing some ten feet ago, I turned around and went back, thinking that if nothing else, I would move the corpse onto the grass where it could decompose in peace.

Grasping the most accessible part of the creature – the tail feathers – I lifted, only to be surprised by a small flutter of movement. I set the bird down and gave it a cursory appraisal: definitely alive; blood coming from the beak, which was intact; definitely in shock. Right, then, back to the house for a little tender loving care.

After years of asking Sam the Vet Tech countless probing questions, I have learned one thing above all else: *always treat the shock*. Shock will kill an animal just as it will kill a human, and if you know nothing else about critter care and feeding, know this: *you must treat the shock*. The underlying injury may end up killing the critter, but there's no reason that shock has to.

It's a simple thing to diagnose: if an animal that would normally bite you and run away doesn't, he's in shock. If it's your own pet and he's completely non-responsive – to the point where he doesn't blink if you touch his eyeball, he's in shock. And shock is something you don't need eight years of veterinary school to treat. You simply need heat.

I avoid heating pads myself, as an animal could chew through the electrical cord and do considerably more damage than the original injury. Instead, I rely on the sort of heat sock that you can microwave and regulate the heat according to the needs of the critter. Most don't need much. A mere *hint* of heat, a suggestion of it, is more than enough, and I considered this now as I stuffed the sock into my own microwave and adjusted the setting.

When the heat sock reached the desired temperature, I wrapped it in a towel – as a further guard against over-heating, created a nest next to the sock with still another towel, then set the bird on the nest. I closed the lid on the container (the same Mouse House that Mice stayed in during his recovery), put it in the closet and shut the door.

The cats, as usual, were very interested in our visitor. It was not an interest that I encouraged. They never *seemed* to mean any harm, but all that looking and sniffing only served to exacerbate age-old instincts and I saw no point in borrowing trouble. Buddy, for one, possessed a keen interest in woodland creatures – the smaller the better – to the point where he was able to fiddle with the closet door until it opened just enough for him to slip inside, hide under a dresser and stare out at the convalescing critter. I actually have to block the door with furniture to keep him at bay.

My first phone call was to Sam, who advised me to allow the bird to rest undisturbed overnight. Birds, she informed me, are touchy beings, easily stressed by contact with humans. I confess it took every ounce of my willpower to refrain from peeking into the closet or otherwise fussing over the bird, but my restraint apparently paid off: next morning, he was alive, awake and alert, if somewhat subdued. I wasn't convinced that he was ready to be released, but he was definitely ready for *something*, so my second phone call was to Wild Haven Nursery.

Because they do such a fine job of lovingly rehabbing wild animals, and because they had willingly taken a batch of abandoned baby wrens off my hands the previous summer, I bore no grudge against the folks at the Nursery over the injured raccoon. I understand that everyone has their limits, and the Nursery's happens to be possibly-rabid raccoons. In any case, they could not have been more helpful now as the woman in charge of these things attempted to assess the robin's injuries over the telephone.

"He doesn't *look* lopsided," I answered hesitantly, "but he's not behaving as I assumed he would."

"Not acting high-strung?" she inquired.

"Right," I replied, "very calm, not jumpy or nervous."

"Better bring him in," she advised.

Having no experience with matters avian – and not wishing to acquire any – I did as the woman suggested. The folks at the Nursery looked the robin over and decided that he had some bruised muscles. After a few days of rest at their facility, he was well enough to be released into the wild.

For the twelve hours that the bird was in my care, he never uttered a sound. Not a peep or a cheep or a trill – nothing. And yet, he still spoke to me clearly enough that I understood what he needed. This is the nature of Critterspeak, the ability to allow the sights and sounds to wash over you like rushing water in a brook, absorbing for yourself merely the *essence*, not the water itself.

The robin no more opened its bill and spoke English than the ducks do, but if you stop waiting for words that will never come, and simply allow the noises to filter in, your brain will usually unscramble them for you. In the case of the ducks, all they ever seem to say to me is, "Kelly!" But *Kelly!* is not a name to them, it's a word with a certain depth of meaning. When they say *Kelly!*, what I hear is, it's *agreeable to see you again!*

Of my four cats, Junebug is the most vocal. This does not mean that she maiows more than the others – that would be Muffin's job. It means that each of Junebug's squeaks packs considerably more meaning in it than that of the other three. Muffin makes demands; Spanky wails unhappily; Buddy says nothing – to the extent that on the rare occasion when he does maiow, I invariably confuse the speaker as someone other than Buddy; Junebug carries on conversations:

"Junebug, you're having a bad morning, aren't you?"
Yeah, Kelly, bad!
"Do you think a snack might help?"
It might, Kelly, it might help.
"Maybe even more than one snack?"
Yeah, Kelly, more!

Junebug will often ask me to play with her at inconvenient times, times when I've just settled down to a meal, or a good book. Her squeaks take on such a pitiful, heart-rending quality that they cannot be ignored:

You play, Kelly!
"There are three other cats here, Little Mitten. Why don't you play with them?"
They're boring, Kelly, they sleep all day.
"That's what grown-up cats are s'posed to do, Junebug."
You play, Kelly!

Wild animals rarely, if ever, talk to me. I believe the only reason that my gang of domestic ducks do is because they're basically hard-wired for a gregarious, farm-animal kind of life. They have neither the self-preservation instincts of migratory ducks, nor the natural sense of reserve that keeps the wild mallards at a distance: while the mallards stay well out of grabbing range, the Pekins are in my face every time. To the best of my recollection, no mallards have ever spoken to me. By the same token, the chipmunk I rescued never actually spoke to me either, but when he finally did talk, he fairly shouted.

I discovered him lying in the chicken coop driveway, curled up in a ball. There was no outward sign of injury – indeed, the Sam and I both surmised that he might simply have been dropped by a hawk. He was completely un-blinking and non-responsive. Even when I held him in my hand and stroked his fur there was no movement. The only indication that he was alive at all was the faint rise and fall of his chest. I took him inside to Meister General Hospital.

Sam always cringes when I launch into one of my rescue stories. While she invariably ends up repeating the same refrain – "I would've done the same thing" – she starts off much differently. She always grills me on what made me think the animal was in shock, and reminds me that in Vet Tech School, it was drilled into the students' heads that you must *never* pick up a squirrel/raccoon/grizzly bear, for fear of being bitten by a rabid critter. Thinking that there must be some overlapping in the symptoms of rabies and shock, it finally occurred to me to ask what, exactly, the symptoms of rabies were.

"The animal's behavior is altered," my friend informed me, "so a raccoon that would normally run away from you might approach you in a friendly way instead." I chewed on this bit of information for a moment, then leveled a frown at her.

"But that isn't the same at all, is it?" I asked with a rising sense of exasperation. "It's an entirely different situation when you have an animal that doesn't move – doesn't even *blink* when you touch its eyeball – and when you have one that's up and walking around and approaching you, isn't it?"

"Well, *yes*," she conceded.

"Then why do you put me through these things, getting me all worked up and fearing for my life like that?"

She gave me one of her sheepish smiles and said, "Just tell your readers to be careful with wild animals, o.k.?"

In any case, I set the little fellow up in the Mouse House, complete with heat sock and towel nest, and into the closet he went. "Chip*muks*," as Spanky calls them, are a particular favorite with him, and he was especially keen to assist me in my ministrations with this one. He spent a lot of time nosing around the periphery, lurking and sniffing and poking his head into the Mouse House when my back was turned. Once the closet door was closed, though, Spanky was forced to move on to other things.

I checked on the chipmunk several times during the course of the evening, and each time found him in varying degrees of distress: sometimes, he was in the same condition as when I initially found him, and sometimes he moved about, burrowing under the towel when he saw me coming. Sam explained to me later that it's typical for an animal to waver in and out of shock for a period of time, and that the best course of action is continued heat and rest.

From my friend's lessons, I established my own recovery criteria: before an animal is fit for release, he must, during his stay at the Mouse House, eat and poop. By morning, the chipmunk had accomplished both of these tasks.

Just outside my kitchen window stands a box elder tree. Instead of one large trunk, there are actually five smaller ones, all growing out in different directions. Underneath the tree is a feeding station of my own devising, something I created with a view to keeping the cats amused, where I distribute sunflower seeds and ears of corn. Chipmunks, squirrels, and birds come from....well, if not *miles* around, then certainly from yards and feet away, running over from underneath the steps of the caretaker's house next door, or from the garage across the forecourt, to fill their cheeks with snacks.

The feeding station was the obvious choice of release site, and I carefully carried the Mouse House outside when I knew that the landlord's dogs wouldn't be around to interfere. Gently, I tipped the plastic container onto its side, aiming the opening toward the box elder tree. The chipmunk hesitated briefly, taking stock of his surroundings. Then, as if he couldn't believe his good fortune, he ran out into the world, launching himself directly at the tree.

What happened next is better than any fiction a writer could dream up, for the chipmunk raced up one branch of the tree, stopped three feet up, then turned and ran down to the base before racing three feet up another branch, then returning yet again to the base and running up still a third branch. A few feet up that branch, the chipmunk turned, ran down to the ground, completed one full circuit around the base of the tree in what can only be described as a victory lap, jumped once into the air with an emphatic, "*Chip!*," and then he was gone, disappearing under the steps of the caretaker's house.

His joy had been palpable, and a far better gift than any *thank you* he might have offered. And with sentiment as powerful as that I had just witnessed, who needed words anyway?

After my seventh suicide attempt, I spent two weeks in a hospital psych ward. It was actually the best vacation I've ever had in my life. My fellow loonies and I would gather in the smoke room (for not even a hospital would deprive its whack-jobs of their cigarettes) and <u>laugh</u> – oh, how we'd laugh! Safe behind those locked ward doors, we let our guard down, and recognized in our mates the same agonizing pain that we ourselves suffered.

Sometimes, we'd laugh so hard, for so long, that nurses came peeking through the window in the smoke room door to see who was feeling good enough to make merry. Hospital thinking was, if you felt good enough to laugh, then you felt good enough to go home. They missed the point entirely: laughter was the <u>beginning</u> of healing, not the end.

Ducks and Lawyers

In fall, the ducks became wary and skittish. It was an attitude they would maintain until spring. While they were in no danger whatever of being hunted, they seemed to possess an instinctive understanding that, for their brethren elsewhere, now was not a good time to be a duck, and they behaved accordingly: in summer, a sneeze from me warranted little more than a glance. In winter, they would rise into the air *en masse* and fly to the middle of the pond, the non-flying domestics flapping their wings and quacking in panic as they ran toward the water, where they would remain until I left. It happened every year.

In a way, their nervousness made my job easier: on the iciest winter days, with single-digit wind chills, I simply wasn't up to the task of sitting patiently on the ground, skin exposed as I tossed bare handfuls of corn. Instead, I adopted an abbreviated winter routine wherein

I squatted down, quickly tossing corn while offering up a running commentary to give them a familiar focus ("Where's Pretty Lady? Look at Big Boy Hovering up all the corn! It's crazy with corn, here, ducks! There you are, Lady!"), before retreating to the warmth of my car to thaw out.

My main concern that winter had to do with the fountain the City had installed in the pond a few years earlier. When the fountain was working, it kept a sizeable area of the pond from freezing. The ducks were not only able to swim and bathe in the most frigid of temperatures, but they also had the familiar safety of the water to retreat to if they felt threatened. But the fountain *wasn't* working, and as the mercury dropped and the air got colder, the pond began to freeze over. I took a small garden shovel with me, a couple of times, in a useless attempt to create a hole, but the ice was thicker than I could manage.

For lack of any better ideas, I upbraided the City in a letter to the local paper, writing that a working fountain seemed a small price to pay for a flock of ducks who added such a pleasant bucolic note to the neighborhood. Evidently, someone at City Hall read my words.

Just before Christmas, I pulled into the boathouse parking lot to find a City truck parked on the beach. A City worker sat inside, staring intently out at the ducks. I tapped gently on his window and made polite inquiries. What he told me set me on edge. The City had hatched a two-pronged plan, which involved:

1. Installing a temporary aerator to create an open area for the ducks while the proper fountain – apparently broken – was removed and repaired, and,

2. Catching all the domestic ducks and sending them to a "farm," then allowing the pond to freeze over completely.

This last was to discourage the thousands of Canada geese, who stop at the pond every year to rest and poop on their way to somewhere else. Evidently, they cause a toxic amount of poo to build up in a pond that people will ultimately be swimming in, later in the year. Which was all well and good but for my ducks who, while I was learning of the "farm" plans, had retreated to the middle of the iced-over pond.

Before I arrived, the City worker had set out a cage, in an effort to trap my guys, and I was hugely relieved to see that they had been smart enough to perceive the danger this man and his cage presented. The worker had, in fact, already given up hope of catching them, and was now simply waiting for a colleague who had gone off in search of a larger drill with which to break up the ice.

I wandered far away from the man and his trap before I set up shop with my bag of corn. All of the ducks – save for one of last summer's babies – waddled across the ice for a meal. The baby appeared to be stuck somehow, but I was far too distracted by what the City worker had told me to consider the possibility of an ice-bound duck. It was December twenty-first – almost Christmas, and I had an appointment in two hours' time. When that appointment was finished, so, too, would the workday be. If I was going to do something about the City's plan, the time would have to be now.

The first lawyer I talked to had handled my husband's divorce. From me. I chose to keep that fact to myself as I explained the reason for my visit. He listened respectfully, and then told me that a pending litigation against the City prevented him from taking my case. Instead, he sent me up the street to another firm, then called to tell them to expect me.

The City needed to leave my ducks alone, I told the next lawyer. The City needed to be a little afraid of animal lovers who could afford litigation. The City, I stated emphatically, needed to know that they weren't omnipotent. The lawyer listened. He quoted a price. He offered his opinion. And he suggested that I take some pictures of the City workers trying to trap the ducks. The lawyer would chew on the problem and get back to me. I raced home and grabbed my camera.

By the time I returned to the pond, the City workers had drilled a hole, installed the aerator, packed up their trap, and left. Now, all the ducks were paddling happily in the water – all but one baby who appeared to be stuck on the ice.

Her feet scrabbled at the ice but she couldn't seem to get a purchase on it. I couldn't tell whether her belly was actually frozen to the surface, or whether it only looked that way – she was too far out for me to see well. I walked around to where the pond was still solidly frozen and stared out at her. Gingerly, I stepped on to the ice and bounced up and down a few times, testing my weight. This is what we did, as kids, on the creek behind my childhood home: you bounce on the ice and it breaks, it's not a good day for skating.

But the ice betrayed no tell-tale cracking sounds, no sloshy-water-just-below-the-surface noises. Inwardly, I drew a breath and a blank – there was *no way* I was walking that ice out to the middle of the pond. And there was no other choice *but* to. In a sort of mental compromise with myself, I knelt down on all fours and wiped away a slash of snow with my mittened hand. Peering down into the ice, I saw nothing but layers of suspended air bubbles. *Three inches thick,* the City worker had told me. It had been in the ten-degree range all week; of *course* it's frozen.

Slowly, I crawled forward, wiping away another slash of snow every three feet or so and peering again down into the ice. I inched along in this fashion, looking no farther than a few feet away or ahead of me. To look further would have caused a sort of horizontal vertigo. I listened intently for the sound of cracking, breaking ice, and heard nothing. Slowly, I moved closer to the duck.

Toward the middle of the pond, I looked up to check my progress. *My God! If this ice breaks, I'm dead!* Standing by the boathouse, staring out at me, was a boy of about ten. A few feet away from him stood a woman with a cell phone in her hand. *There's a crazy lady out on the ice,* I imagined her saying into the phone, *better bring a straight jacket!* Well, there was nothing for it now but to continue the mission.

As I neared the baby – who apparently chose this moment to not recognize me – she started to panic. Making frightened squeaky noises and scrabbling again at the ice with her feet, she tried in vain to get away from me. The closer I got, the more fearful she became until, with one last desperate look over her shoulder, she willed herself – by dint of sheer terror – to escape by using her wings. The poor girl literally *winged* herself across the ice, her belly sliding along like a cross-country skier propelling herself solely by using her poles. It must have been an excruciating effort.

I crawled along behind her for a few yards, shouting words of encouragement to keep her moving: she was so close to open water now that if she stopped and got stuck again, another rescue attempt would be far too dangerous. When she finally cleared the ice and dropped into the water, I turned and crawled back to terra firma. The woman and boy were gone now, and I was left to dust the snow off my pants before I dashed off to my appointment. As I drove up the street, I passed a boy of about ten who turned, saw me and saluted. I couldn't help but smile at his obvious stamp of approval.

Reaction to my madcap escapade on the ice was divided between those in the "helping" profession – who tried to impress upon me the folly of risking my own life to save that of a mere duck, and those who possessed a modicum of faith in my overall sensibilities. Sam's comment on the subject was, *in toto,* "I would've done the same thing." That's not what the therapist said – in fact, quite the opposite.

In addition to my regular shrink, I'd been seeing a woman who did EAP – equine assisted psychotherapy. It was cutting edge stuff, at that time here in the Midwest, and I was keen to see how yet another species of critter could help me in my journey toward wellness. Unfortunately, while the horse was great, and the therapy a good idea, the woman herself was one of the most useless, issue-addled therapists I've ever come across.

She wasted an entire session out at the horse barn lecturing me on priorities, and telling me in no uncertain terms that risking my life for the sake of *any* animal was unacceptable. After chewing on her words for a week or so, I went into her office and told her that my priorities were my own, and that her *lecture* was unacceptable. I dumped her soon after. When the shrink has more obvious problems than the client, you know it's not going to work out well.

What fate awaited the rescued duck and her kin, I had no way of knowing. To keep myself from going crazy with helplessness, I began a ritual of twice-daily drive-bys, pausing in the boathouse parking lot long enough to count heads and reassure myself that my gang of ducks were still safe.

Over the Christmas holidays, the lawyer found time to draft a letter to various members of City government. He made deft use of the information I had given him: I, too, had been busy during the holidays, telephoning assorted Federal beauracracies and animal welfare agencies, trying to ascertain what rights – if any – abandoned domestic ducks might have in a situation such as theirs. As it happened, the only protection afforded to my gang fell within the purview of some rather vague animal cruelty laws, but it was entirely unlikely that the City administrators knew this.

Accordingly, the lawyer quoted this man from the Division of Wildlife, and that woman at the Humane Society, knitting together a letter which seemed to contain a wealth of information on animal rights and welfare, but in reality consisted of very little in the way of usable ammunition. It was all we had, and we gambled on the unlikelihood of the City wanting to be seen as animal bullies. I approved the proffered copy and the lawyer sent it off to City Hall. He expected a quick response.

The City's response was quick in more ways than one. Apart from delivering their letter to the lawyer the very next day, the letter itself was terse and to the point. We were informed that the City had abandoned its plan to move the domestic ducks, and that they considered the matter closed. *Why are you bothering us with such a ridiculous issue,* they seemed to ask.

The City administrators clearly wanted to put as much distance between themselves and the Crazy Duck Lady as possible. I could just imagine the dialogue, "Someone paid a lawyer good money to write *this*?" The City's attitude was fine with me: their distaste for the issue meant that my guys got their reprieve. At the time, though, I had no way of knowing just how short that reprieve would be.

And Then There Were Five

The only reason I was in that particular neighborhood at that particular time was because I was in the middle of a meltdown. Well, it isn't called *Sane* Critter Lady, now, is it? I had phoned my therapist, requesting an emergency session, and she'd found me an hour near dinnertime. It was as I pulled into the parking lot that I spotted the cat huddled under a car. I had arrived a few minutes early, so I put the time to good use trying to coax the cat to come out to me.

She was a small grey tabby with an injured front leg, but her coat was clean - a sign that someone had taken care of her – and it didn't take much encouragement for her to come out and, hobbling in three-legged fashion, circle cautiously around me. I made a gentle grab for her and scooped her up into my arms, unsure whether I was hurting the injured leg. She put up a small amount of fight, struggling in a half-hearted way and issuing a few perfunctory maiows. I snuggled her close to my chest and spoke soothingly as I made my way back to my car.

I had, as always, a modest complement of rescue gear in the trunk: a critter carrier, a thick woolen blanket, the ever-present shovel. It was the carrier I hoped to get at, but I was reluctant to take even one hand off the kitty for fear she'd escape. Lacking any ideas, I eased open the passenger door and climbed in backward, so that my back rested against the dash, and my knees were propped against the seat back. The door was mostly shut against the cold winter evening. We sat that way for some minutes. As I relaxed on the car seat, the little tabby closed her eyes and began to purr. I sensed in her a strong feeling of relief.

When the shrink got out of her own car, I waved her over. Explaining the situation, I popped the trunk and waited while she fished out the carrier. I had no trouble depositing kitty into it, and as my therapist is also an animal lover, I brought the cat inside with me. Once ensconced in an office, I gave her the run of the room while the shrink and I talked.

It was she who pointed out that we were nowhere near a residential neighborhood, although the fact that we were just two blocks away from the local Humane Society raised plenty of questions. We surmised that perhaps the cat had been dumped *at* the shelter, as opposed to *in* it.

I planned to take the kitty to the Humane Society at the end of my session, but by then, they had closed for the day. Knowing that my friend Sam was still at work just up the road, I called and made boarding arrangements; I would take the cat to the shelter in the morning.

Things were going more or less according to plan (with the small but notable exceptions that, 1. Dr. Green thought the gimpy leg was permanently damaged and, 2. someone else at his office thought the cat was pregnant) right up until the young lady I dealt with at the Humane Society told me that they had reinstated their kill policy – a policy wherein animals were euthanized for being "unadoptable," or simply taking up space for too long – and that Little Gimpy's prospects weren't all that good. The girl never came right out and said so, but she let it be known that pregnant and disabled were not good things to be in a shelter already over-run with unwanted cats.

All the while we talked, the knocked-up cat in question lay quietly in the carrier. I had set the thing on the counter, opened the door and stuck my arm inside as a gesture of reassurance. My hand was resting on kitty's back as the girl tried to be delicate about the idea that Gimpy might not last the day.

I looked in at her, this small bundle of fur who was lying there, curled up on a towel with her eyes half-closed. She looked completely unconcerned, as if she had every faith in me and my ability to take good care of her. Me, maybe – but clearly my local Humane Society wasn't going to.

I huffed in irritation as I closed the carrier door and took kitty back out to the car. After the experience with Tommy, I knew that I could at least get this one spayed – maybe even for free like last the last one – so I took the cat back to Dr. Green's, figuring that I could buy myself some time to make a few phone calls while she recuperated from the surgery.

As it turned out, the rescue group I called could barely manage to pay a portion of the spaying: it was almost the end of the year, and their budget was mostly depleted. Still, they paid for half the cost and that was something, and as kitty rested, I spent time making half-hearted phone calls to rescue groups who couldn't take her anyway; there were simply too many others in line ahead of her.

Well, I knew that I would take her even before I admitted to myself that I would take her. Sam knew it, too, though she said nothing. The twinkle in her eyes was enough to tell me that she was on to me. I realized it was definite when I found myself bothered by the working title I had given her, "Gimpy." It seemed a frivolous, disrespectful name for a cat who had laid so trustingly in the carrier, a cat who kept even her bad leg meticulously clean. A cat who conducted herself with such dignity. Clearly, she needed a name to suit who she really was, and without much difficulty, I settled on Gracie. Unfortunately, the name wasn't going to mean much to the gang at home, who had no idea what was coming.

I was more worried about Gracie than the others. I had no idea how she would feel about being thrust into a home where four cats already resided. I made a space for the carrier in the laundry room near the litter boxes; she could use it as her safe haven for as long as she wanted. I set small dishes of food and water near the carrier door, and then left for an appointment.

By the time I returned, several hours later, she had abandoned the carrier in favor of an upholstered rocking chair. For a time, the house was divided into two areas: Gracie's end, which meant primarily the kitchen, and the rest of the house for the rest of the cats. Parity would eventually be reached, but each had to get there in his or her own time, and some took longer than others.

I was surprised that Spanky was the first to extend the paw of friendship, but I shouldn't have been. Spanky had thrived in the "you're my favoritest cat" environment, and had finally found his place in the family again. He understood now that no new kitties could change the fact that he was the bestest, specialest cat *ever*, and so he made himself gentle, and available, and didn't hiss when Gracie came near. It was a generous gesture, and I made sure that Spanky got extra helpings of love from me in return.

Buddy spent some time making it very clear to the interloper that he was the man of the house. This involved doling out occasional smacks to Gracie's head for no apparent reason except to show her that he could. I let him get away with it for a week or so, and then I reminded him who was the boss of *him*. Junebug seemed unsure of what to do, and so mainly did nothing. She did assert herself in the one area that mattered to her most, my lap.

Junebug is not a lap cat by nature, but she does have one exception: when I'm on the toilet. She'll catch me there several times a day, always jumping up and settling in for a visit. It's our time, and Junebug treasures it as much as I do. Patiently (because Junebug doesn't care that I need to stand up and get on with my day), I'll tell her how pretty her brown eyes are, remind her of all the parts of her that resemble her Big Cousin Cats (her cheetah face, her snow leopard paws, etc), and I'll sing many refrains of the Junebug Song. This is a little ditty of my devising, sung to the tune of *I'm a Little Teapot*, and not something that I am inclined to commit to paper; I'm not that crazy.

In any case, when I reassured Junebug that our toilet routine would not be changed by the presence of the new kitty, she seemed to relax. Within weeks, I saw her tentatively trying to play with Gracie. Ultimately, they would end up at night sleeping one on each side of my pillow.

It was Muffin who threw a fit – a *big* fit, hissing in disgust at every opportunity. The mere sight of Gracie hobbling down the hall sent Muff into paroxysms of rage, and while I wanted Muffin to feel that she had a voice in the family, she was taking things way too far. Even when I reprimanded her, she continued to growl and hiss as she scuttled away. There was nothing for it but to let it run its course: Muff had, after all, started out life as an only cat, and her indignation was understandable.

As for Gracie, she held her own. The main reason that the other cats spent several weeks at the opposite end of the house was because Gracie fought back. Unlike Junebug, who took all the abuse they threw at her, Gracie wasn't taking crap from anyone. Once they'd all retreated to the living room, Gracie would choose her spot – always some place warm and cozy – and *sleep*. She slept so much I began to wonder if something was wrong with her, but I sensed nothing more than an ongoing, blissful relief. Occasionally, she played with the toy mice, but for the most part, she preferred to nap. Perhaps sleep had been a luxury in her previous life.

Her leg would have to be dealt with. Fortunately, it was not a pressing problem, so there was no hurry. Dr. Green's initial opinion had been to amputate at the shoulder, but after spending some time watching Gracie play, I saw that she had movement and ability in most of the leg. Basically, the wrist and paw would need to go: they were frozen in an awkward position, and dragged uselessly on the ground. But the remainder would be good for gripping large toys and other cats, so it seemed unfair to deprive her of it. When the time came, a surgical strategy would be worked out with Dr. Green, a man whom Sam said was the best veterinary surgeon around.

In the meantime, with five cats but no husband or children, I now qualified for official Crazy Critter Lady status. Any day now, I knew my membership card would be coming in the mail. Every time someone asked how many cats I had, I winced. When their eyebrows rose at the answer, my response was always a shrug and, "I *meant* to have two…," implying that I hadn't the vaguest idea how those other three had gotten in the door.

Red's Gift

It is an unfortunate fact of life that children have a tendency to grow up and leave home. Having no offspring of my own, save the cats – who only want to go out in the garden and catch mice – I've never had to suffer the pangs of sadness that Sam has. Just the other year, her middle daughter tied the knot in a flurry of lace and roses, leaving me sitting on an uncomfortably hard wooden church pew, reflecting that there was *no way* you could pay me to be that young bride's age again. The very next year, when Red's beau proposed and the chaos of wedding planning ensued, I shook my head at the madness of it all and thought privately, *just because he asks, doesn't mean you have to say yes....*

But Red saw things differently, and as the clock wound down to the Big Day, the reality of the situation began to sink in: *Red would be leaving for good!* My friend seemed to take this imminent second loss in stride, but the thing nagged at me in an admittedly selfish way: Red had helped me navigate the unfamiliar world of computers, when I wrote my first manuscript. Unable to afford my own computer, I had asked if I might come to Sam's house and use hers. In keeping with her generous nature, my friend reminded me where the key to the back door was located, and told me to make myself at home.

Thus began a routine which carried on for over a year: coming on the days that my friend had to work, arriving an hour or two before she left, I settled down in front of the techno-monster, half-listening to the chatter from my friend, and half-focused on the task at hand. I invariably ended up entertaining everyone within ear-shot with my agonized groans, and the off-color insults I hurled at that confounding mass of microchips. At one exceptionally low point, I even managed to delete my almost-finished manuscript – an event which would have ruined me completely had Red not already taught me how to save things on disc.

Red taught me loads of things that year – all without the slightest complaint or hint of impatience. She didn't even seem particularly amused by my ignorance. Unfail-ingly charitable and kind, Red answered every question, and came to my rescue every time I screeched. In retro-spect, it was probably the path of least resistance for her, but I was eternally grateful and said my *thank-you*'s every chance I got. Then, just as I was contemplating having another go at that beastly computer with a new manu-script, it hit me like a brick in the face that the next go would be entirely different, for in a matter of months, Red would be gone.

In a mild panic, I asked Sam, "Isn't there some way you can put a stop to this?" In one memorable e-mail, I suggested that my friend put her husband to work building a small cell, er, *room*, in the basement, complete with "an unpickable lock, and good sturdy bars on the window." But my ideas fell on deaf ears and the wedding plans steamed ahead, leaving me unhappily in their wake. Meanwhile, I had the matter of a gift to consider.

For the past few years, Sam's three daughters and I had conspired to get together for a photo session – usually in the fall – at which I would spend a very agreeable span of time taking group photographs, one of which always ended up tucked under the family Christmas tree.

My friend had a fair idea of what's going on, but as I know the work schedules of both her and the Mr., I was always able to slip into the house a week before the holiday and position the end result of those happy fall photo shoots in some unobtrusive spot beneath the tree. Sam always finds a prominent place to hang these pictures, and I understand now that when those rotten little monkeys began their exodus, my photos took on an additional significance: they may be leaving, but for that one click of the shutter, they're all together again, smiling and carefree.

A picture seemed to be the obvious choice for a wedding gift now, but of what? I had already taken loads of engagement photos of the happy couple, and a proper professional would record the event itself. By the time the Big Day was over, they would be awash in photographs. If I was going to contribute to the stockpile, it would have to be something *really* good - exceptional, even. Something no one else had thought of. Then it came to me: who were Red's two favorite men in all the world? *Her beau and Obie!*

My elation at having come up with the perfect wedding gift was quickly tempered as some portions of that computer-time chatter with my friend came back to me: dimly, from the tangled mass of spaghetti that is my befuddled brain, I recalled talk about the beau, a mild-mannered chap named Nathan…Nathan and Obie… Nathan didn't *like* Obie?...Nathan was *afraid* of Obie.

Oh, dear.

I asked him anyway, figuring, I'm touting this idea as a surprise for his intended, what choice does the poor guy really have *but* to say yes?! Which is, of course, what he did – and quite gamely, too, although I did soften the request a bit by reassuring him that he didn't actually have to stand on the same side of the fence as the horse. To my everlasting surprise, he set a date for the shoot a couple of days hence, when he knew that Red would be away.

Unfortunately, the day greeted us with the remnants of a hurricane which had traveled several hundred miles to dump its drenching rain on our plans. When I called Nathan and left a cancellation message, he surprised me again by calling back within the hour and setting up a time for the very next day. *Either he really wants to get this over with, or he really loves Red,* I thought wryly, *possibly both.*

He arrived promptly on the day. Always liking to know whether I have to hurry through my paces, I asked if there was any place that he needed to be afterward. In fact, he was required to be at a location some twenty-five minutes away, in the direction he had just come from, in an hour. I showed him the bag full of cut up apple chunks with which I intended to bribe Obie, and explained to Nathan how to hold his hand out flat when feeding them. Obie was nothing if not consistent in his willingness to be bribed, and I felt certain that this fact would be the key to our success.

I told Nathan that I'd heard some talk about him that I wanted to clarify, and I asked him to choose a word which best described his feelings about Obie. I even tossed out a few to get him started. "Afraid?...intimidated?...love him with all your heart?"

"I would say 'nervous,'" Nathan replied earnestly.

"O.k. Any particular reason?"

"Obie's a big animal," he stated matter-of-factly.

Well, he wasn't wrong.

We walked out to the barn, and I showed Nathan where I wanted him to stand – on the *outside* of the fence, as promised. Then I fetched Obie's halter and lead rope and disappeared into the stable. I gave Obie a couple of apple chunks to get him started as I slipped the halter over his head. With a *tsk*, we were off, heading to the stable door some five paces away, where Obie apparently decided that he'd had enough of this walking stuff and resolutely refused to take another step.

I don't fancy myself a horse expert, but I *have* learned a few tricks to use on stubborn horses. The only thing is that the stubborn horses I've used them on were just uncertain enough to concede that I *might* be the alpha horse – at least while I was waving my arms and shouting emphatically at them. But cranky old Obie made no such concessions, so I left him where he stood and walked over to where I'd left the bag of apples, announcing to Nathan along the way that, "This might take a bit more time than expected," to which he replied, "Here he comes now." Naturally, when I looked back over my shoulder, there was Obie strolling amiably across the paddock in our direction. Once he got a look at the size of the bag of apples, he was more than willing to cooperate.

I can't say that I know much about Nathan. In all the times I've been to Sam's house, we've never really exchanged more than a greeting. He seems a quiet, steadfast type, small of stature but no doubt long on character. He had stood supportively by Red through a number of health crises, and even somehow managed to find an indulgent streak in himself with regard to animals: apparently not terribly fond of *any* critters, he'd had to learn to contend with not only Red's horse, but the indoor dogs and cats, and the multitude of barn cats, as well – all of which Red took at least a cursory interest in.

But Nathan was no match for all those creatures, and I think he knew it, and found that the path of least resistance was simply to *stand still* in the middle of the rushing critter waters, and let them wash around his ankles.

In any case, he stood in position near the fence, outwardly calm as I handed over the lead rope. His steady resolve seemed to waver just a little, though, when I tried to hand him some apple chunks. "I'll let you give him those." He said it so calmly that it took me a moment to realize that he had just – very deftly – deferred to me a task which would have required him to touch the horse. And to touch the horse would have involved standing closer to Obie than Nathan cared to be, for he had staked his claim to a spot a couple of feet out from the fence, and a couple of feet back from Obie, and he wasn't budging.

I had had it in my mind's eye that the two would be standing close enough to each other that it would almost look as if they were nuzzling heads, but that clearly wasn't going to happen, and I could see that the situation was going to require a certain photographic ingenuity to even get man and horse in the same *frame*. Fooling with the camera angle bit, I was able to shorten the distance between them and create the illusion of intimacy. It was the only way to hide the fact that Nathan - for all his efforts to appear casual - was indeed afraid of Obie.

We got through the roll of film without incident. I would snap a couple of pictures, stopping occasionally to adjust my perspective, and to give Obie more apple chunks and a scratch between the ears. He stood look-ing philosophical about the whole thing and I won-dered if he could detect the apprehension in Nathan. If he did, he gave no indication, and simply continued to stand quietly and munch his snacks. I told Nathan that we only had a few more frames to go.

"He's behaved very well," I remarked, as I looked up at Obie appraisingly, "would you feel at all comfortable moving a little closer?"

Again, the brief twinge of unease, and then, "You mean?...like...*here?*" as he took a micro-step sideways toward the fence. It brought him no nearer to Obie than he'd been before.

"Well, maybe a step forward," I suggested.

He took a micro-step forward, then, which put him essentially four inches closer to the horse. I let it go at that and finished up the roll of film. Thanking him profusely, I told him that he was free to go, and I mean to tell you, *he went.* I turned my back to address Obie, and when I turned around again, both Nathan and his car had disappeared from the property.

In the twenty-odd minutes we'd spent on this endeavor, from asking Nathan to clarify his feelings about Obie, to the deft manner in which he'd hidden his trepidation, I never once laughed at Nathan, or made fun of him. Even in the telling of the story to Sam, who was equally amused by his stoic determination to do this thing for his bride, I managed no more than a fond smile, and I'll tell you why: because while he could just as easily have said no to my request, Nathan chose instead to put himself in an uncomfortable position simply because he knew the photo would make Red happy.

Once the gift project was out of the way, I turned my attention to Obie himself. For all of her twenty-three years, Red had lived at home. For the past thirteen years, Obie had lived there, too. Even after they'd stopped competing, Red still attended to Obie every single day. She mucked out his stall, fed him, groomed him.

She didn't have to spoil him with snacks, just being together was enough: I'd seen her effect on Obie, how he would stand there while she brushed him, utterly at peace in her presence, his eyes half-closed. He had no way of knowing that soon, Red would cease to be a daily anchor in his life, but *I* knew, and I was determined to see that he didn't get lost in the wedding frenzy.

I don't know how these things come to me, I just know that they do. One minute I'm lying in bed trying to fall asleep, and the next, I'm giggling over the details of some newly-hatched plan. So it was one night a few weeks before Red's wedding, as I lay there plotting the details of Operation Obie.

Once the idea came to me, I exchanged a series of e-mails with Sam, secretly working out the most opportune time to hatch my plan. Sam liked my idea, but worried that Red would be too stressed out by wedding-day jitters to appreciate the effort. Privately, I disagreed. Red wouldn't have much spare time on her hands on the Big Day, but she always had love in her heart, and I felt certain that she'd understand the gesture. Besides, if Red was going for good, it was only right that Obie help send her off.

Several days before the wedding, I went to the local craft store for supplies. I stocked up on poster board, markers, and pipe cleaners. I spoke to an employee about my plan, and she showed me the perfect ribbon for my scheme – an open weave thing that looked like burlap, with gold thread running through it. She even created a horse-sized bow with the stuff. I took everything home and spent a happy couple of hours putting it all together.

On the morning of the wedding, I made my way to Sam's house. Red and her bridesmaids were off getting their hair and nails done. She stayed in constant communication with Sam, so I knew exactly when to expect her return. I spent the intervening time working on Obie.

In spite of my excited tone of voice, Obie had absolutely no interest in the plan. His boredom continued even when I invoked Red's name, and I practically had to drag him to the cross ties. Once there, he stood moodily while I curried and brushed him, making sure he was spotless.

When I finished grooming him, I wrapped the burlap-looking ribbon around his neck, and secured it with the pipe cleaners. The bow hung jauntily on his right side, just out of nibbling range. I poked two holes in the top of the poster board and attached it to the ribbon; the sign hung under his neck. Sam came out to inspect the finished product, and stood grinning while she told me that Red's ETA was five minutes.

It's never an easy task getting a thousand-pound animal to move when he doesn't want to, and, of course, Red's wedding day was no exception for Obie's usual obstinance. He was far more interested in doing a little lawn mowing than he was in doing my bidding, so I pulled out my secret weapon – a bag of carrots.

Once he realized that snacks were involved, Obie perked up considerably. He lumbered over toward the driveway and we stopped a few yards away. Once in place, we stood and waited. Sam hurried inside for her camera, and as she returned, the car bearing Red and the bridesmaids turned into the drive. Red was speaking to one of the girls as she got out of the car, so it took a moment for the sight in front of her to register.

Red had spent many months orchestrating this day, down to the smallest item. She's the classic example of a first-born stickler for detail, and here was her mother's weird friend throwing a wrench in the works, if only for a few minutes. For standing in front of Red was I, wearing a grin from ear to ear and holding on to her beloved Obie, who was wearing a festive golden-burlap bow around his neck and a sign that read: *DON'T FORGET THE HORSE!* To her credit, the harried bride managed a grin of her own, and even posed for pictures.

After over a decade's-worth of therapy, I still feel weird. I <u>am</u> weird. No one else I know comes up with goofy ideas like gussying up a horse for a wedding he wasn't even invited to, or takes a proprietary interest in a pond-full of ducks. Maybe I was meant to be weird. If there hadn't been an abusive childhood, maybe I would've turned out even weirder.

I used to want to be "normal." It was actually my therapy goal for a few years. But the closer I got to it, the less I wanted to be it: normal seems so bland, so conformist. So grown-up and dull. Forget that! Give me talking cats and quacky ducks any day.

Operation Relocation

On a sunny day in April, I was busted. Unbeknownst to me, Whoville's Animal Control Officer – a mild-mannered guy named Dave, stood several yards behind me, watching quietly as I immersed myself in happy conversation with the ducks. "Good morning, ducks! Just look how fetching you are today, Pretty Boy! And there's Big Boy! It's a lovely day to be a duck," and on in this vein, completely oblivious to the fact that I was probably being overheard. I love the ducks, but the details of our conversations are not something I want getting around.

It was when I stood and turned to leave that I became aware of the officer's presence, and I feigned a nonchalance I didn't feel: feeding the wild mallards – who invariably joined the gang and I - is against the law, and surely this particular member of the City police department knew that. As it turned out, he wasn't there to haul me away on felony duck-feeding charges.

He remarked on the ducks' trust in me, then told me that he had been tasked with removing them from the pond. He wondered if I would be willing to assist him. Sensing an opportunity to steer the project in a direction which would satisfy me, I decided to help. By the time we finished talking, Officer Dave had agreed to let me choose the ducks' new home, *and* the date of the move – which, because they were nesting, would be some vague and unspecified day in the future. At the time, I had no idea that I had just undertaken to do the impossible.

I made any number of phone calls, during the spring, and spoke to any number of people who were able to put me in touch with other resources, but who were not able to find me any specific homes. No one wanted these ducks who had no rights, who could not fly, and who seemed boring by comparison to the cute puppies and kitties that the shelters had in overabundance.

The season *did* buy me some time: both Pretty Lady and her daughter, Brown Duck, were sitting on nests, and Officer Dave agreed that we should wait until the ducklings were hatched and grown before we moved them. So I had plenty of time on my hands to work on Operation Relocation, which I needed, as the phone calls weren't getting me anywhere. In the meantime, I had been encouraged to continue my feedings and, in fact, Officer Dave went to the trouble of informing the boat house staff of my 'authorized' presence.

While Brown Duck (the one I rescued from the ice the previous winter, who would acquire the proper name of "Mama" once her ducklings hatched) stayed mostly on her nest, Pretty Lady came out to feed every time I appeared. Her choice of nest location was an unfortunate one: she poached an old nest situated beneath a pine tree near the boat house. It was an old tree with airy branches, making the nest very easy to see, and within a short amount of time, virtually *everyone* – dogs, children, the boat house staff – knew she was there.

Because *I* knew that Lady's nest was there, I would set up shop about ten feet away, calling to her as I unpacked the bags of corn and bread. Sid and Sol would quack for her to join us. So would her beau, a small mallard who, having seen the three large ducks move in close and Hoover up the corn, came to be fairly fearless of me, too.

Lady would quack from under the tree. Looking over my shoulder, I could see her tucking up the edges of the nest, taking care to cover the eggs before she left to come feed. It was the same routine day in and day out, and I took her quacks to mean, "Save some for me! I'm coming!" When the eggs were covered to her satisfaction, she would race toward me as fast as her webbed feet would carry her, coming to a stop directly in the middle of the pile of corn and exclaiming, "I've been sitting on that nest forever! *I'm hungry!*"

When the time came for Lady's eggs to hatch and nothing happened, I began to grow concerned. It was about this time that some neighborhood children pointed out Brown Duck's nest to me. Even I hadn't known where that one was. As we stood looking at Mama and the tiny nippers who peeked out from under her feathers, the children told me they had seen teenagers taking eggs from Lady's nest and throwing them. I was sickened; that breaking duck eggs could be construed as entertainment saddened and disgusted me.

As I was digesting that news, an unleashed dog – who appeared to know exactly where he was going – ran toward the pine tree and directly at Lady, who squawked and ran to the water. The dog chased her, running right across the nest, breaking at least one egg in the process. When I hollered *you bad dog* at it, the owner apologized, thinking that I was upset for myself. Then he smiled and told me that his dog liked chasing ducks. "I'm guessing *she* doesn't care for it much," I replied curtly as I gestured toward Lady, who had –thankfully – escaped the mutt.

Ultimately, *none* of Lady's eggs hatched, and Sam – who is, among her other qualities, an eternal optimist – suggested that perhaps the eggs had never been fertilized to begin with. Glumly, I shook my head no: I had seen one of the thrown, broken eggs. Part of an almost-fully-formed duckling spilled out from the shell. At night, lying in bed and running through my usual list of things for which I owed the Gods a debt of gratitude, I made numerous pleas for the souls of those destroyed ducklings; their needless loss broke my heart.

Brown Duck, who had carried on such a discreet courtship that I had only guessed at her nesting until the children showed me proof, produced ten ducklings, eight of which would survive to adulthood. Owing to her rather unusual light brown coloring, her young were even prettier than Missy Miss's festive bunch. Several of them were a creamy off-white color, flecked with brown and grey. There was even one duckling that looked like a smaller version of Mama.

Brown Duck, who had always been a bit reserved with me, seemed to let her young make up their own minds. The vibe I got was a sort of, "If you want to get near the Big Thing, be my guest." As they grew in size, the ducklings grew, too, in courage, and just a few weeks after their birth, they all ran within inches of me as they pecked at corn and evaded the pokes of the grown-ups.

The highlight of the feeds – and what a highlight! – was when Mama's babies would spot me from the water. The minute they heard me calling, they began to *peep-peep* in excited anticipation, racing toward me through the water as fast as their tiny feet would paddle them. It positively melted my heart when I realized that they were peeping for *me*.

In the meantime, I had approached a local apartment complex, which had on its' property a fair-sized lake, and two large Pekins already in residence. I showed the youngish manager-ladies a photo of the ducks – one taken during the previous winter's panicked headcount – and asked if they might have room for a few of the gang. The answer was an enthusiastic 'yes.' Problem solved. Sort of. I didn't actually *want* to move my guys. And every time I spoke with Officer Dave, he seemed more and more reluctant to commit to a definite moving date.

I decided to drum up a little publicity for the ducks, phoning a reporter for the local newspaper and suggesting the ducks as a story. This could not have been a more opportune move on my part: I learned that the reporter I had spoken to was an animal lover, and her husband had recently joined the board of the local Humane Society. I poured my story into her tape recorder and offered to let her use some of my duck photos, as well, but curiously, before the story even went to print, Officer Dave had a change of heart.

I can't say whether that change of heart had to do with Officer Dave's friend, the City's Director of Important Things, who ultimately offered to keep an aerator going all winter for no other reason than that he liked the McKinnon's Pond ducks, or whether it was simply a matter of practicality, but somewhere along the way, Officer Dave apparently concluded that scaring away the unwanted geese by shooting blanks at them periodically would be the path of least resistance. His conclusion could not have been more timely.

A couple of months after our initial conversation, I stopped in to touch base with the enthusiastic duck-lovers at the apartment complex. Noting that one of their ducks appeared to have gone AWOL, I made inquiries, and the answer chilled me. I was told that someone had decapitated one of the ducks, and thrown both the head and body into the lake. I was aghast. I sympathized with the distraught owner – a young woman who told me that since the slaughter, she had tried without success to retrieve the other duck and move it to a safe location. Bitterly, she advised me to take my ducks elsewhere, a conclusion I had already reached.

It was when I reported that horrific act of cruelty to Officer Dave, and told him that the ducks would *not* be moving there, that he asked, rather hesitantly, "Well, couldn't they just stay where they are?" – as if moving them had been my idea all along!

Despising the helplessness I felt at the plight of that poor terrorized duck, I took pen in hand, in a letter to the local paper, and challenged the resident Christians – who had been remarkably vocal about not being allowed to say a prayer at a school graduation ceremony – to step up to the plate with the far more relevant issue of animal cruelty. God's most vulnerable creatures need you to defend them, I wrote, and condemn those who would hurt them. They were all I had, my words, and they wouldn't bring that poor duck back, but maybe they would help protect my gang, who, upon learning of their latest reprieve, merely quacked at me agreeably and requested more corn.

CatsPlay

Unless the former chicken residents were exceedingly clean, and required a laundry room, then the structure I live in was never actually a chicken coop. My theory is that a coop once stood on this site, was razed, and a house built on the already-existing cement slab. I have never confirmed this, though, as it would require a conversation with Lord and Lady Witless, a thing I was keen to avoid unless absolutely necessary.

Regardless, my home has the *shape* of a chicken coop, and was built to accommodate the very long rectangular slab. In fact, the distance from the hall closet, at one end of the house, to the entrance of the living room, at the other end, is roughly forty-seven feet. The hallway floor – a fake brick linoleum that I would really like to replace, makes a superb skating rink for cats and humans.

When Winkie was still alive, and we lived in a cramped apartment, I used to dream of the day when I owned a house with an acre or so of land. On bike rides around Whoville, I would survey various properties, stealing for myself their landscaping ideas, and embroidering on a fantasy of mine to create a backyard run for Winkie.

It would be low-slung, completely enclosed with chicken wire, and would run the length of the yard. I would plant evergreen shrubs alongside it and as they grew, they would provide discreet cover for the critter-stalker inside. Winkie would be able to hunt as he pleased without actually being able to *catch* anything.

But of course, it was not to be, and one of my bigger regrets when he died was that I hadn't been able to provide him with anything beyond our tiny apartment. Many's the time I've walked my chicken coop hallway, wishing Winkie were still alive and able to enjoy its numerous possibilities. Sometimes, even now, *Always with you, Kelly!* rings in my head as I ruminate on what he's missing, and I hope that he's right – I hope that he *is* somehow enjoying that 47 feet-worth of hall.

Buddy certainly is. When he's all wound up, he likes to get a running start down near the bathroom, race past the bedrooms, kick it up a notch as he enters the living room, then use his momentum to springboard off a cat condo by the back wall up on to a decorative valance that hangs above the window. Peering down at the minions below, he's clearly very pleased with the fact that he's the only cat in the house able to perform this impressive feat.

For Muffin, the hallway is mandatory exercise: her favorite chair is located at one end of the house, while her favorite hobby – eating – is at the other. Muffin is a fat cat who porked out by sneaking kitten chow meals when Winkie was a baby. Even after several years of dieting, she's lost no more than a couple of ounces.

Dr. Jill once tried to console me by saying that it's almost impossible to get a cat to lose weight, and that two ounces was actually a considerable achievement, but I refused to be placated. Despite my determination, though, Muff hasn't lost so much as a microgram since, which is a little strange when you consider that she's getting quite a workout every single day.

The cat who gets the most out of my hallway is Junebug. Several times a day – whenever she catches me doing something useless and unacceptable like relaxing at the kitchen table – she'll plant herself in front of one of the cabinets. Combining significant glances upward – where the snacks are kept, with impassioned squeaks, she lets me know exactly what she wants: *You play, Kelly!*

The game involves me standing at one end of the long hallway and tossing treats for her to chase. These snacks are of the low-fat, low-fun variety, but the cats seem to like them anyway. Since the calories involved don't amount to much, I feel free to dole them out in generous quantities. Typically, I'll throw treats to varying distances, requiring Junebug to dash this way and that, running, jumping, and gleefully skating the length of the hall. It's terrific fun.

It's at those times more than any others that I become aware of the inadequacies of language: as Junebug anticipates my next snack toss, I can sense in her a feeling, a state of being for which there is no translation. The closest I can come – a group of words so utterly lacking in descriptive value as to make a mockery of the joy I sense, would be, *you're the bestest playpal ever, Kelly!*

Sometimes, Spanky joins the game. Because Junbebug is such a shamelessly greedy soul, it's necessary to divide the playing field in half, with me at the fifty-yard line. Snacks fly in one direction for Spanky, and in the other for Junebug. It seems to be a mutually agreeable arrangement, as no one gets shortchanged in the process. Every now and then, Buddy – and even Gracie – will join in. At that point, it's a juggling act, trying to ensure that everyone gets a piece of the action.

There's a rather curious aspect to that hallway. In ordinary circumstances, the curiosity would be considered a baseboard. In this instance, though, the builder got entirely carried away with regard to size: while the baseboard on one side of the hall is a relatively normal five inches high, with virtually no measurable depth, the baseboard on the other side stands a whopping seven and three-quarter inches high, and juts out two and a half inches from the wall. I have no idea why.

The thing doesn't seem to serve any purpose at all, and beyond using it to expand my dust collection, I was at a loss for what to do with it. After two years of living in the chicken coop, I finally came to see that little ledge as a cat-sized storage shelf. Tired of picking up the myriad fake mice and milk carton rings every time I wanted to sweep the floor, it finally occurred to me to store them on the ledge.

At intervals down the length of that hall, at perfect cat's-eye height, ranges the entire collection of toys. All a browsing cat has to do is look and sniff and make a selection. And while I've never seen them in the process, it's clear by the scattered toys I awake to that the cats have done just that.

The arrangement never fails to amuse Sam. Virtually every time she stops in, she pauses in the entry way, casts her gaze down that hall, points, and laughs. It's as if she's seeing it for the first time, every time. Sam doesn't have the advantages of a jutting, otherwise useless ledge in her home, and since the larger of her two dogs enjoys nothing more than the occasional fake-mouse snack, she's forced to keep the cat toys hidden until the dogs are sent outside.

The minute they're gone, Otis – who is, among his other special qualities, Junebug's sibling – will jump up on to the side table and give the sugar/flour/coffee container lids a nudge. Because those lids are ceramic – and therefore *heavy*, they do nothing more than *clink* back into place. After hearing a succession of *clink*s, it dawns on whoever is present to remove the lid and let Otis have at the contents. He'll poke his head inside the canister, select a mouse, carry it down to the floor and play happily until he sends the thing skittering under the fridge.

Both Sam's cats and mine have reaped the benefits of my catnip-growing hobby. This started out some years ago with two cats and one plant. I expanded the number of plants considerably when I discovered the stuff growing wild around an abandoned house in the neighborhood.

Unsure whether the owner – who lived, oddly, right next door to the empty house, would object to someone pilfering his useless weeds, I conducted an undercover operation, skulking about at sunset. I nabbed four fair-sized plants, raced home and put them in the ground, then repeated the process and nabbed four more.

It was, of course, completely ridiculous to concern myself with the idea of misdemeanor trespassing convictions, but I find that a small dose of paranoia always seems to heighten the satisfaction.

After a summer spent studiously ignoring the plants – save for the occasional dowsing with Miracle-Gro – I ended up with an impressive crop that filled three one-gallon plastic bags. It seemed to me more than a little sinful to save it all for the cats – even if there were now five of them. I spoke with my alterations lady, a fellow cat-lover named Dolores, who kindly agreed to donate her sewing services if I bought the fabric and stuffed it full of catnip. Between the two of us, we made over seventy catnip-filled toys, 98% of which were ultimately donated to my favorite critter charity, Best Friends Animal Society.

While she worked, Dolores would occasionally update me on her progress, embellishing her reports with tales of how her ancient cat would suddenly spring to life and offer to help. It was the same with my five, whose volunteerism varied from Muffin's explicit demands for a cut of the goods, to Buddy poking his head into every available bag and container in search of the treasure, to Junebug's goofy attempts to roll around on the pins and needles. Everyone got seriously stoned, and none among them could see the value in containing the 'nip in a pouch of fabric, let alone giving the stuff away. Junebug was the most intractable on this point, and protested often, *But Kelly! We could have it!*

No amount of explanation about underprivileged cats in Third World countries could sway Junebug's opinion; as far as she and the others were concerned, giving away perfectly good 'nip was a monumental waste. Fortunately, the day I moved the box of toys from the closet to the car, with a view to shipping them out to Best Friends, all five cats were enjoying a group nap. They never noticed a thing.

CritterSitter

There are those instances in life when the Gods decide to smile on you for no apparent reason. So it was one wintry February when Sam asked if I would look after her critters while she and the family were away. She might just as well have invited a kid to go crazy in a candy store – it would've produced much the same effect. Immediately the words left her mouth, I began plotting the many ways I would spoil Obie the horse in her absence. There was, I recalled, a box of particularly distasteful granola bars gathering dust somewhere in my kitchen. There were also a number of burrs stuck to his body that I was itching to get at. But first, there were practical matters to contend with.

Before the family left, I went out and followed my friend around on her morning chores. The two dogs would be boarded, which actually made no dent in the number of critters I'd be looking after. Sam spent thirty minutes or so walking me through her routine, showing me where the bird seed, the barn cat food, the horse pellets, and the hay were located, as well as the treats with which she placated an impatient Obie. His water bucket would need topping off daily, and naturally, the water spigot had a personality all its' own.

The water supply for the property came from a well, and the handle for this particular spigot rose up out of the ground no more than eight inches. You had to turn it *just so,* then pray to the Gods to bring forth water, and if you were lucky, they would comply. But even as Sam outlined the procedure and filled two buckets while I watched, I knew that the minute the family drove away, that spigot would give me fits. I wasn't wrong.

I followed my friend in, out, and around the barn, watching as she demonstrated how to muck out Obie's stall, and where to toss his hay. I was enormously flattered that she – indeed, the entire family – trusted me to take good care of their thousand-pound animal. The cats were easy: it didn't really matter that there were over fifteen of them, they all ate the same food regardless. They lived in and around the barn, and were accustomed to an unrestricted life. Obie, on the other hand, was a huge responsibility, with a complicated anatomy, and the potential for small problems to turn deadly in a hurry. You don't want just any old slob in charge of that.

So I listened intently to everything Sam said, carefully sorting the information into various categories: *Stumpy likes to knock over the birdfeeder while you're trying to fill it* (minor); *if any of the cats look sick, go ahead and take 'em in to Dr. Green* (keep an eye peeled); *I'll leave the number for the equine vet* (yikes!). In fact, she left phone numbers for every contingency, along with a box of cinnamon graham crackers, a six-pack of bottled water, and a spare key to the house. With that, they were gone. And not a moment too soon, either, as the weather was due to take a turn for the worse. But first, there was Thursday.

In order to appreciate my enthusiasm for Thursday's weather forecast, it is first necessary to understand that the average high temperature in Northwest Ohio in February is thirty-two degrees. This does not take into account the wind chill factor. For those of you who are unfamiliar with such things, the wind chill factor is a little thing that gauges what the air feels like when the wind is blowing. Because when the wind is gusting at 25 mph, it no longer feels like thirty-two degrees, it feels like *two*. In such breathtaking cold, the wind will shear the cornea right off your eyeball, if you're not careful, or at the very least, it will exfoliate your skin in a manner that you did not intend.

Because Sam lives in a rural area, the wind chill factor is a vital component of the weather forecast. There are no windbreaks to speak of on or near her property, so when the wind blows in winter, it blows hard and cold enough to take your breath away – and that's the least it will do to you. But Thursday would be different. On Thursday, the forecasters claimed, the sun would shine, the birds would sing, and the temperature would soar to the mid-fifties. And for once, they weren't wrong.

It was a beautiful day – and it would be the last for some time. I took full advantage of it and spent two happy hours grooming Obie. As the sun shone down on us, I curried all the dried mud off him, and then brushed his coat until it gleamed. After that, I set about picking the burrs out of his mane and tail – he seemed to have rolled end-over-end in them – while Obie contentedly munched hay. When I finished, he was one pretty horse.

The barn cats enjoyed the sunny day as much as Obie and I, coming out into the paddock to mill around our feet. There was Timmy, Momcat, and Mosette, Beebins and Bobbins, Stumpy and Bocephus, and several others whose names escaped me. Some asked for attention, while others preferred to commune from a distance. To a one, all were clearly grateful for the unseasonably warm day.

It was much too good to last, of course, and in fact, the forecasters were predicting a rather sobering turn of events: for the weekend, highs in the low twenties, with gusting winds. Indeed, Saturday's wind chill factor put the temperature at something like five degrees.

I wasn't unduly worried about this. I'd had the good fortune, a couple of years back, of stumbling upon an exceptionally warm down-filled coat at a garage sale. They had asked ten dollars for the thing, which I considered fairly extortionate. On the other hand, I knew I'd never get a coat of that quality for ten dollars in a store, so I plunked down the money and took home the coat. It looked as if it contained the feathers of a thousand geese – a bit excessive, really, unless you live in Reykjavik – and it was actually uncomfortably warm on all but the iciest days. Now, I knew, was the time to pull the thing out of the closet and dust it off.

I can't say that I was toasty warm out there in the savage cold, but between the extra socks, the long underwear, the scarf, the hat, *and* the thousand geese, I was comfortable enough to spend thirty minutes or so going over Obie with the brush each day. In that weather, I thought I might as well give him all the advantages of a clean coat. Besides, he made a pretty good windbreak.

There would be no more communing with cats, after Thursday. They all decided to wait out the wind huddled in the barn, and who could blame them? They were understandably unhappy about the weather. Obie, though, was becoming unhappy for a different reason: he missed his people.

The novelty of the warm weather on Thursday, coupled with the lengthy grooming from me, had distracted Obie to the extent that he didn't realize the family was gone. By Saturday, he'd figured it out, and voiced his displeasure in the most obvious way he could think of: he banged his food bucket against the wall.

Over and over, harder and harder, he banged that bucket, until I became seriously concerned about damage to horse or wall. I reached into his stall and gave him a reassuring pat on the neck, for which I got a glare and flattened ears in return. I understood: since his competition days ended, Obie had quietly retired to the back forty. He had nothing to do all day but graze, roll in burrs, and visit with the family. It wasn't much of a routine, but it was *his* routine, and he was obviously distressed about the disruption to it.

I didn't bother trying to explain it to him – it wouldn't have changed the situation, and Obie didn't care about *why*, anyway. He just wanted things back the way they were. There was nothing for it but to sympathize, and steer clear of the parts of him that could hurt me; Obie's not a *mean* horse, but he *is* an ornery one.

Instead of taking out his frustration on me, he turned his flattened ears to one of the cats who had followed us into the stall, and I had to use my *I'm-the-boss* voice and warn him, "Knock it off!" The rare times I used that voice, Obie always looked startled and immediately quit what he was doing. This time was no exception, and in fact, he seemed a little hurt: *you didn't have to yell!*

The wind blew so fiercely that weekend that it knocked over the family barbecue grill. I found it lying on its' side next to the water spigot which, by Sunday, refused to work. I turned the handle this way and that, muttering oaths at the Gods and even giving it a few whacks with an errant grilling tool, but to no avail – the thing was frozen solid.

I sighed in resignation, knowing that from here on out, I would have to trudge up to the house, fill the buckets in the family bathtub, then trudge back out to the barn. It was a small thing, really, and the family would be home late Monday night, but the brutal cold had taken the shine off the fun of looking after my favorite horse, and under all those layers of clothes, I was a little tired.

Every night, the wind knocked at least one of the bird feeders out of the tree, and every morning, I struggled in that wind to find a more secure branch for it. This was my best friend's home, and I wanted to care for it just as she did; she would do no less for me. So I kept a sharp eye on which barn cats turned up for dinner, and which seemed sick or disinterested. I kept track of how much food went into Obie's mouth, and whether it came out the other end. I put out as much bird seed as Sam did, and scooped every pile out of the indoor cats' litter boxes. I even turned off a couple of ceiling fans that Sam had left on, just to be safe.

And, because I'm such a sucker for critters, I stood out in that perishing cold grooming Obie every single day. This last was actually no chore at all, but the high point of my visits. But you can only do it for so long before the cold starts to wear you down.

I kept a daily journal for the family, noting the highs (*he's burr-free!*), and the lows (*I'm gonna have to fill 'em in your tub!*). I wrote down which cat had maiowed the loudest, which cat seemed under the weather, and at the end of the last entry, I asked the family to take note of Obie's reaction to their return, as I was fairly certain that he'd be one delighted horse. Indeed, I heard later that he danced a little jig.

It was typical of Sam to give me my own key to her house. Even when I pointed out that I already knew where the spare was kept, she felt it would be more practical in the long run for me to carry one on my key ring. Trust is not something I take lightly. Indeed, I'm always exceedingly flattered to learn that I've earned it. It was one thing when my friend trusted me to simply work on her computer and not loot her home in the hours between when she went to work, and an offspring came home from school. It was quite another thing to be given my own key and entrusted with the care of a zoo's-worth of animals for five days.

It was also a mark of how far our friendship had come, from our first years as client and veterinary staffer.

Slowly but surely, we built a friendship based on our passion for animals. Carefully, we picked our way through the minefield of philosophical differences, concluding that the critters were more important than who was in the White House, and this is where it's brought us: to a place of mutual respect, and an understanding of just *why* the other deliberately throws herself in the path of helpless animals, even when we *know better*, and can't afford it. She has a key to my house, too.

In a curious turn of events, the next time I was pressed into critter sitting service, the weather swung to the opposite extreme. Now, instead of bone-chilling cold, the forecast called for highs in the upper nineties, with commensurately high humidity. It was the mid-western equivalent of a Brazilian rainforest, except without the piranhas. Solace lay in the fact that Sam and Farrell maintained a swimming pool: above-ground, relatively shallow, but a cooling body of water nonetheless.

You're probably thinking that summer critter-sitting involves little more than a t-shirt, shorts, and flip-flops, but you'd be wrong. In the first place, marauding gangs of mosquitoes rendered even *Deep Woods Off* fairly useless. The more clothing I wore, though, the harder it was for the bloodsucking little buggers to get at me. Experience taught me to wear jeans – no matter how hot they made me, and douse not just skin, but t-shirt fabric as well, with bug spray.

Then there's the matter of footwear. The fact that Obie's stall and arena are veritable minefields of dung notwithstanding, you'll have to imagine for yourself what it would feel like for a thousand-pound animal with sharp-edged hooves to stand on your bare foot.

Since *I* can imagine that scenario pretty vividly, I choose to wear a good sturdy pair of boots with thick woolen socks whenever I'm around horses. So, taking care of Sam's zoo in a sweltering heat wave was no simple matter. There were bugs to be battled, and critters to be made comfortable before I could even *think* about hopping in the pool.

The indoor cats had it easy: tender-hearted Sam had left the window air conditioner running for them, despite considerable opposition from Farrell, who was not inclined to pay the electric bill for cold air that no human would be enjoying. As a compromise, she set the AC for 80 degrees – a temperature that *might've* been comfortable if we weren't currently in the heart of the Amazon. But with the sort of heat that produces illusions of oases and harems, an air conditioner running at 80 degrees offers no relief at all.

I suspect it was Otis the cat who changed the setting. I saw him lurking more than once in the vicinity of the window in question, and I noticed that as the outside temperature got higher, the AC setting slowly got lower. At the height of the heat wave, the temperature inside the house dropped five degrees. With such suffocating heat nipping at our heels, I didn't have the heart to chastise Otis, so I said nothing – though I made sure the setting was back at 80 the day the family was due to return.

The barn cats dealt with the heat as best they could. Most found cool spots here and there around the property, and simply settled in, waiting for the worst of it to pass. Each time I approached the barn, Momcat – an orange and white cat of immense proportions – would poke her head up out of some cooling clump of weeds to see what was happening. She appeared to have staked out a number of cooling clumps of weeds because she was never in the same place twice. Very few of the cats were interested in eating in such scorching heat, so I merely topped off the dishes of kibble, knowing they'd eat in the evening when it cooled to a relatively-frosty 78.

It was Obie I worried about the most. Fat and sluggish, there was no relief for him but the stale shade of his stall. No breeze ran through the stall to cool him, there was merely the lack of sun beating down on his back. So every day, I spent ten minutes blasting him with a hose. This was terrific fun for both of us – for me, because his pleasure was obvious, and for Obie, because not only did he get to cool down considerably, but he also got to roll in the dirt, afterward.

Sam had told me how, in his competition days, Obie had to be tied up after a bath because the first thing he wanted to do was lie down and muddy up in the dirt. Obie didn't understand about looking pretty for the judges then, and I didn't care about it now, so at long last, he was free to do what came naturally. I'm not sure which he enjoyed more – the hosing or the rolling.

Hosing Obie down came to be a bonding experience. As I ran the spray over his body, I kept up my usual commentary about how pretty he was, and how special. He would stand motionless, soaking up the water as well as the praise, and learning in the process that he could trust me to not spray water in his face.

There were times when standing around being spoiled made him thirsty. Instead of walking over to his water bucket, Obie would search out my hand, and we developed a system: gently, I'd spray water into my hand,

and Obie would lap it up. I've hand-fed dogs and cats and ducks in my time, but never before had I watered a horse by hand. It was a surprisingly intimate act, this huge animal so delicately licking water from my hand with his enormous tongue. We would stand face to face for a few minutes, looking deeply into each other's eyes. And then he would try to use me as a scratching post.

Owing to the marauding gangs of mosquitoes, Obie had itchy spots in places he couldn't reach, like his chin. Ordinarily, he would avail himself of a fencepost, but I guess he thought I would serve the purpose, because he took to rubbing his chin back and forth across my shoulder. When a thousand-pound animal pits his weight against a 130-pound weakling, it is of course the weakling who buckles. And so I did, dodging out from under his head and protesting, "Ob! I'm not a fencepost!"

Not everything ran smoothly. An ancient cat who had wandered in a while back was looking pretty haggard. A shot of steroids had been discussed, but I assumed that Sam hadn't had time to take care of it before the trip. I called her and left a message, asking whether she could arrange for someone from Dr. Green's office to come out and give the injection. Sam called back and left her own message, saying that she *had* given the shot, and if the cat – Smokey Bones by name – seemed sick enough, then I should take her into the office and have her euthanized. *I trust your judgment completely,* said my voice mail. Yikes!

Fortunately, Smokey Bones wasn't quite that sick, and with a little encouragement from me, she ate a surprising amount of kibble, then set about doing some grooming – both good signs for a sickly cat. While I appreciated Sam's vote of confidence, I didn't want anyone dying on my watch. So I was happy to spend the necessary amount of time in a virtual steam bath, coaxing a sick cat to eat, and cooling off a pudgy horse. And when all the critters had been taken care of, *then* I'd jump in the pool.

Trust matters. The first, worst lesson my parents taught me was that humans can't be trusted. Animals have their own trust issues: wild critters figure it's better to be safe than sorry, and will flee almost every time, no matter how benevolent your intentions.

Domestic animals vary, each according to his personality, and previous contacts with humans. In my opinion, domestic critters are optimists: they _want_ to trust you, and they're generally willing to give it a go.

Critter trust is precious to me. It means I've passed the test, respected the boundaries, and consistently displayed the requisite calm and patience. I trust them, too: I trust my cats not to shred my skin when we play; I trust cranky old Obie not to act from a place of malice. I wish humans could be so easily trusted.

Planned Duckhood

In my searching of websites to learn more about domestic ducks, I noticed a prevailing theme: duck over-population. Any number of web pages made dire predictions about lakes and ponds being strewn with rotting corpses – the result of too many ducks and not enough food. The main problem is the large ducks' inability to fly away once the food source has been depleted. As I watched my gang slowly but surely increase their numbers, I began to see what the websites were on about, and it became obvious that *someone* would have to do something about it. Naturally, that someone would be me.

The previous fall, I consulted Officer Dave on the matter, telling him I thought it would be best to remove all the eggs I could find, come spring. Dave countered by suggesting that I shake the eggs – in effect, *scramble* them, then leave them in the nest. If you take the eggs, he explained, the duck is liable to lay more.

Egg stealing, I could handle. Egg scrambling was another matter entirely. Egg scrambling was way too dramatic – not to mention *traumatic* – for my squeamish nature. There was just no way I could do it.

So I turned expectantly to Sam, who had assisted Dr. Green in countless spay and neuter surgeries over the years. Surely someone who had effectively helped Dr. Green perform kitty abortions wouldn't have any trouble with egg shaking. While Sam grimaced over the details, it must be said that she was far more stoic than I about doing what needed to be done. I told her I'd be on the lookout for nesting ducks, and would let her know when it was time. Grimacing once again, she nodded her assent.

Come spring, it wasn't hard to tell who was nesting. Pretty Lady and Brown Duck both seemed to take forever to turn up for feeds, and some days, didn't come at all. Because they were both lazy and predictable ducks, I had little trouble finding their nests – well, Brown Duck's, anyway; Lady's took a bit longer to find. I almost walked right into Brown Duck's nest, located as it was just five feet from last year's spot. In it were eleven eggs.

I had startled Brown Duck when I trampled through the bushes, and she jumped off the nest and ran a few feet away. She stood under a nearby tree, waiting for me to leave as I squatted over her nest, frothing in a lather of indecision: Sam's schedule was such that by the time she'd be able to come out to the pond, those eggs would be much more than just yolk, they'd be ducklings. And shaking the eggs then would be too horrific to contemplate.

Realizing that it was now or never, I took a deep breath, held an egg up to the sun to make sure there was nothing duck-like inside, then methodically began to shake. Afterward, I set each egg down on the ground, to keep track of the *before's* and *after's*. It took a very short amount of time to shake them all. When I finished, I carefully placed each one back in the nest. It had been a disturbing – albeit *necessary* – task.

It appeared that Pretty Lady had chosen the same awful nesting site as the year before, but I soon realized that the three eggs lying exposed to the elements weren't Lady's eggs. These eggs, slightly smaller in size than domestic duck eggs, had been stolen from a nearby wild mallard nest by thoughtless neighborhood children, and placed in that old nest for reasons only an idiot would understand. It actually took me a few days to figure out where Lady's new nest was.

The gang had done their weird territorial thing again – they did it every spring – in which Sid, Sol, and Lady hung out on one side of the boat house, and the rest of the ducks were relegated to the other side. Interlopers were sent scurrying by Sid and Sol, and the boundaries were, for the most part, respected. I pulled into the lot and parked on Pretty Lady's side, easily spotting the two white Pekins as they lay on the grass in unusual proximity to a nearby apartment building. The apartments were a stone's throw from the pond, and I knew that wild mallards had, in the past, availed themselves of the shrubbery in front of the buildings for nesting purposes. Now, it seemed, Lady had, too.

The Pekins watched as I carried the bag of cracked corn down to water's edge, but they did little more than walk around in circles, quacking softly. It was several minutes – the time it took Lady to cover her nest – before they all came running to feed. I dumped the corn into a pile on the ground, moved a couple of feet away, then squatted down to commune for a bit. I was pleased that Lady had chosen a decent nesting site this time, something tucked unobtrusively into boring shrubs that children wouldn't waste their time on. I remarked, "I didn't know you had that kind of sneakiness in you, Lady, hiding your nest like that!" She made no reply, but I swear she was smiling.

Since duck eggs incubate for twenty-eight days, and I'd been aware for at least two weeks that she was nesting, it was, in my estimation, much too late to do anything but hope that Lady hadn't laid a lot of eggs. Of course, that hope was dashed when I went looking for – and found – her nest. It contained twelve eggs.

As it turned out, Lady's nest wasn't in the shrubs after all. It was – get this – five feet away from the shrubs, up against the building itself, *right out in the open!* With no protective cover whatsoever, Lady had reached new heights of stupidity, and all I could do was shake my head in wonder. She eventually turned up for a feed with two ducklings in tow. I wondered, then, what had happened to the rest of her eggs, and the answer wasn't long in coming.

Since she'd had no offspring the year before, Lady apparently forgot how to be a good mother: she and the Pekins would wander off in various directions with what seemed like no regard whatsoever for the two innocents in need of protection and nurturing. It was as if Lady didn't care in the least what became of them.

In the meantime, Brown Duck disappeared altogether, along with her look-alike offspring, Junior. There were never any corpses to tell the tale at the pond, and there were none now to indicate what had become of the two light brown ducks. The details would forever be a mystery.

During the new babies' second feed, I found two dead ducklings under a tree. Thinking that cruel children were involved, I availed myself of a local cop who happened to be at the boat house that day. Because the City police department conducts educational programs at the elementary schools, I thought perhaps this officer could add animal cruelty to the curriculum.

To my surprise, he said he had seen the two ducklings in question a day or two before, and that they'd behaved as though they were feeble, or somehow impaired. Apparently, Lady had all but abandoned them, which explained why I hadn't known about them. The cop went on to say that he thought the flightless ducks were a problem and needed to be removed from the pond. While I was searching for the right words to defend the gang, the ducks' savior – Officer Dave – showed up.

During the ensuing conversation, in which Dave told the other cop that my guys were actually *good* for the health of the pond, it transpired that, unbeknownst to the other, Dave and I had *both* been shaking eggs. And, evidently, Dave had been far more thorough than I. We chatted about the various nests we'd found as I walked him over to the dead ducklings. It was Dave's job to dispose of them.

It was the sort of thing he was called upon to do every day, but I sensed in him a measure of sadness over the loss of those helpless little fuzzballs. I remarked to him the irony in the fact that when a duck laid eggs outside the U.S. Treasury, her nest was cordoned off and she got her own guard, but we couldn't manage to give our nesting ducks any protection at all. Dave agreed, "A lot of parents aren't supervising their kids, that's for sure!"

I knew that Lady's two remaining ducklings didn't stand a snowball's chance in hell of surviving the summer; Lady was just too disinterested in being a mom. And since Dave and I had done our jobs so well, there were very few other ducklings on the pond that spring. The ones I did see belonged to wild mallards who kept them well away from humans.

It was an unsettling change. How many bags of corn and bread had I brought to the pond for my gang and their little ones over the years? How many times had I heard the excited *peep-peep* of the babies as I approached? I could count five generations of ducks among my friends. Every spring, there had been new faces, and new personalities to fuss over, take pictures of, commune with, and worry about. Now, thanks to a very necessary population control plan, there was none of that. It cast a considerable pall over the feeds, and for the first time in all our years of friendship, I found myself reluctant to visit regularly.

One element that added considerably to my glum mood was this: I had made certain rules about the timing of the egg-shaking. If I knew that the eggs had been in the nest for a few weeks, I deemed them too far along in their development to shake in good conscience. But based on my conversation with Officer Dave, I don't believe that he made the same distinction. I began to wonder if Dave's shaking the eggs too far along in their growth was what had enfeebled the two ducklings who didn't make it, and the thought saddened me: it was one thing to destroy the contents of those eggs when they were nothing more than yolk. It was quite another thing to destroy a growing duckling, and my early visits that spring lacked their usual joy because of it.

Still, I had undertaken the task of looking after the ducks, and giving up that responsibility was inconceivable. If I needed any reminders as to *why* I had begun this adventure, though, I didn't need to look any further than the eager faces of Sid, Sol, Pretty Lady, Pretty Boy, and all the others who had come to know me: years later, they *still* came running and quacking to greet me, and that was reason enough to keep going back.

Happily, I turned out to be wrong about Lady's ducklings: one baby *did* survive, an intrepid little Pekin I named Peepers. Peepers didn't seem to mind looking after himself, and, indeed, spent so much time alone, or with Sid and Sol, that I began to wonder if Pretty Lady even remembered that he was hers. Every once in a while I'd see mama and baby together, but the lessons Peepers learned about how to be a duck came from watching the others, not his mother.

Every day that I came for a feed, Peepers was a little bigger, and a little braver, and then the day came when he ate out of my hand. Never had a duckling so young been so courageous with me, but Peepers had seen a lot of other ducks do the same thing in his short life. Peepers seemed to be a quick study all the way around: every time I approached the ducks for a feed, I called out

Peepers! as soon as I spotted him. In a matter of days, he was peeping at me in response.

In the meantime, Pretty Lady spent her days sitting on a new nest of eggs. It never occurred to me that she had laid more until the day I arrived to see four little fuzzballs following her. *This is what happens when you mess with nature,* I mused, *they find a way to work around you.* And so she had.

While I was delighted to see a new batch of nippers – the population-control experiment was turning out to be the sort of failure I could happily live with – there was something about Peepers that made him the most joyous addition to the gang. I suppose, in a way, he reminded me of me: he had waged a solitary struggle for survival, and won. Since mama wasn't much help, he turned to others, watching and learning from them instead of giving up in defeat. I admired his tenacity, his cheerful determination to get on with life. And because of that fortitude, he became one of my all-time favorite ducks.

Obie Rides Again

Here's an oxymoron for you: I'm honest enough to admit that I tell the occasional fib. And I told a whopper in the chapter where I first introduced you to Obie the horse: Not looking to ride him?! *Lying my butt off!* Of course I wanted to ride him! But I was told that the laminitis he suffered from occasionally causes horses to be put down, and indeed, the laminitis Barbaro contracted after his injury – and not his broken leg – was the reason that the famous racehorse was euthanized.

The collective sigh of relief the family breathed when Obie pulled through his latest bout could be heard across town. Sam and Red had been badly frightened by the incident, so it was understandable that neither wanted to press Obie's luck by making him *do* anything. Doing nothing has its' own price to pay, though – a fact that Sam eventually figured out.

Given the natural ebb and flow of life, a number of changes took place that, in and of themselves, wouldn't amount to much. Taken together, those changes apparently gave my friend pause for thought. The biggest change, of course, was that Red got married and moved thirty minutes away. Between a new husband, a new home, and a new job, she had little time to devote to the kind of attention she used to give Obie. She still tried to make it out to the old homestead as often as possible, but her new life was slowly replacing the old one, and Obie stopped being the everyday priority that he once was.

The second change was due to the creative genius of Obie's farrier, who cleverly devised for the horse a pair of what Sam called "tennis shoes" – specially designed horse shoes that helped correct Obie's foot problem. The tennis shoes worked so well that Obie now felt good enough to buck around the paddock like the silly old boy that he is.

The third thing wasn't a change at all, but an on-going dispute between Sam and Farrell over the amount of feed Obie was to get each day. Sam showed me the measuring scoop, filled to overflowing with alfalfa pellets. "This is how much *he* gives Obie," she informed me, "and *this* is how much Obie's *supposed* to get." She dumped over half the pellets back into the bin. It was a considerable difference.

But no amount of argument could persuade Farrell to dial down the portion of feed, so Sam cut out Obie's evening meal altogether. Even then, she remained concerned about the food-to-exercise ratio – the overdose of feed, combined with the lack of exercise – which was making Obie very portly indeed. Because excessive weight is a contributing factor with laminitis, you can see the vicious cycle for yourself. And so could Sam.

I made repeated offers to exercise him. I wasn't even talking about riding, but simply attaching a lead rope to his halter and walking him around the property. It would've been more exercise than he got on his own. But Sam always hesitated, and, feeling that Obie was mostly Red's horse, insisted that Red be consulted. I never did get the green light, so I assume that Red said *no*.

Perhaps the biggest change of all had to do with Sam's perception of me. I'd been taking riding lessons for a couple of years by then. Every other Saturday, I drove out to a local stable, climbed on a lazy old nag named Crazy, and took instruction from a girl half my age. Because she'd spent her entire life around horses, I never gave the age difference a second thought: she knew her stuff, and that was all that mattered. After each class, I'd log on to the computer I finally bought and email Sam the highs and lows of the lessons. She's the only woman I know who understands the language, and the passion.

The lessons were about much more than just riding: before I could even put a saddle on Crazy, I had to groom her from mane to tail, and pick all the gunk out of her hooves. I learned to run my free hand over her body as I brushed her, checking for bites and sores that a saddle might aggravate. I learned how to wrestle a hoof away from her when she didn't want to give it, and I learned how to hang on to that hoof when she tried to take it back. The lessons were, above all else, confidence-builders, and as my knowledge increased, so did my self-assurance.

My new sense of confidence began to show in the way I dealt with Obie during visits. I no longer treated him as an endearingly large puppy, but rather, viewed him with the healthy respect that comes with knowing how dangerous a thousand-pound animal can be: all it would take is one leg lashing out in horsefly frustration to split my skull wide open. Obie, like every other horse on the planet, simply has no understanding of his size and strength. Thanks to those riding lessons, I *do* understand.

But while mindfulness was a priority for me, fear was not, and during my interactions with Obie, I operated on the assumption that both of us would be respectful of the other, and not do anything to cause distress. Over time, I came to see that Obie seemed to be operating on the same principle.

I became aware of the change in Sam's thinking during a visit one warm spring day. Peering out the dining room window that overlooks the property, I asked, "Are those *traffic cones* out there?" Sam said Farrell had set them out. *Yeah?*

"Something to do with golf; I think he made himself a driving range." The cones were exactly like the ones Crazy and I worked with during our lessons.

"Cones, huh?" I mused, "I could take Obie out there and walk him around them, give him some exercise."

When Sam replied, "Go ahead, I think he'd like that," my jaw nearly hit the floor! I was out the door before she could change her mind. In no time flat, I hooked him to a lead rope and led him out of the gate.

At the time, it didn't occur to me that Sam would be watching us from that dining room window, but surely she noticed the same thing I did – that Obie's normally-sluggish pace had quickened, that his head was up and his ears alert. *At last*, he must've thought, *something interesting!* It was a pace he usually reserved for feeding time, and his enthusiasm cheered me.

I maintained a running commentary as we walked, to offset any nervousness he might've felt; it had been a long time since he'd left his paddock. "See, Ob? The grass really *is* greener on the other side!" When we reached the far end of the property, I stopped and let him graze a bit before heading off on another adventure: the neighbor's woods.

Sam and I had walked her dogs through those woods countless times, following trails made by time and children. The dogs knew the way by heart, but I doubt if Obie had ever set foot in them. He never hesitated, though, as I led him through the maze of paths – not even when the woodchuck we startled dashed noisily to safety.

It was a terrific beginning, and when I gave an enthusiastic account of the walk to Sam, she dropped a bombshell: "You should start riding him!" It was one of those moments where you say very loudly in your head, "Please, God, don't let her change her mind!" How many years had I been wishing for just one ride? How many times had I heard the phrase, "We'll have to see what Red thinks"? I was stunned.

Fighting the urge to drag Sam to the tack room, I chose instead a more practical approach. I would spend some time working with Obie "on the ground," as they say. I wanted to give both of us a chance to get to know each other, and create a working relationship. I made arrangements to come out and work with him twice a week.

In spite of Obie's initial enthusiasm, though, I would soon learn that he took a perverse delight in pointing out who knew more about horsemanship – and it wasn't me! I wish I could say that all our workouts were as pleasant as our initial adventure, but the fact is that they went from bad to worse in no time at all. The more I asked of Obie, the less he was willing to do, testing me to see if I really knew anything about horsemanship. Between you and me, Obie actually knew much more than I did. I just didn't realize that *he* knew that!

I was used to being tested by Crazy. She had a fondness for refusing to give me her hooves when I asked for them. I would stand there nudging, cajoling, begging, and pleading, trying to pry a hoof up off the ground so that I could clean it, and Crazy would stand there pretending to be deaf. It took me some time to learn the level of assertiveness necessary to gain Crazy's respect, but it never occurred to me that I would have to start all over again with Obie. Apparently, you get a horse's respect one horse at a time. And Obie had no intention of giving it away for free.

Obie's most consistent test was to simply stop walking and refuse to move. This trick was particularly vexing when he did it on neighboring properties: I didn't want those neighbors thinking I was a horse rustler, and I didn't want Sam worrying that something bad had happened to delay our return. Mostly, I didn't want Obie thinking that I didn't have any control over him.

I employed a variety of methods to get him moving – from slaps on the rump, to tugging on his lead rope, to dragging him around in circles, all of which had varying and unpredictable degrees of success. In one memorable instance, Obie got the scent of a neighbor's horse, planted himself in one spot, flapped his lips and made a succession of *nuh-nuh-nuh* noises – the like of which all horses are capable of, but that I'd never heard from Obie before. It took all of my creative resources to unglue his feet that day.

It was around this time that I learned what Obie's *real* name was. Apparently, he had come out of the womb exceptionally stubborn, and an early trainer, frustrated by Obie's attitude, took to calling him *Stubborn Old Bastard*. When Sam and Farrell bought the horse, they didn't want their young children exposed to such language, so they shortened the name to "O.B." Sam says she fibbed to the kids and told them that the initials were short for "Obadiah."

Whatever the name, that trainer wasn't wrong. And while Obie had clearly been a handful long before I came on the scene, I confess that I took some of his behavior personally: here I was, chock-full of horse knowledge – all two years of it! – and yet this cranky old geezer was getting the best of me. I consulted Connie, my riding instructor, who gave me some good advice, and I resolved not to give up. Obie was a smart horse, and a champion to boot. It was only a matter of time before we connected on a working level.

Obie was also a likeable horse, happy to show his appreciation for all the apples and carrots I plied him with. There's nothing quite like a slobbery horse tongue on your arm to let you know that you're held in some esteem! And while his stubborn nature certainly tried my patience, it also made any success I had with him all the more satisfying.

In the meantime, those famous words, "We'll have to see what Red thinks," went the way of the Dodo bird. Sam apparently felt that, whatever deficiencies I possessed as a horsewoman, I knew *enough*. Naturally, Obie heartily disagreed, and made sure I knew it at every turn. Clearly, in his mind, a champion horse having to deal with an insufferably ignorant human was an indignity of monumental proportions.

The day finally came that I felt ready to ride Obie. I had queried Sam on matters of tack – I was not well-versed in the infinite variety of bits and bridles, and I knew I'd need help getting all the necessary stuff onto Obie's back, and into his mouth. Sam assured me that she had been the one to outfit all the horses her children had competed on over the years, and she felt confident that there would be no difficulties in getting his gear together now. Unfortunately, her optimism turned out to be woefully misplaced.

Because my own memory is virtually non-existent, I really shouldn't make any jokes about Sam's. I'm simply going to say that I don't believe she actually *has* one. As the minutes ticked by and Sam continued to fumble with the bit, I began to grow concerned: their youngest offspring was at a friend's house getting ready for her senior prom. At six o'clock, Sam and Farrell would be leaving to go take pictures. Sam had been very emphatic about me only riding when someone was home, so my window of opportunity was slowly closing. 4:00 turned into 4:30, and then 5:00 before Sam got everything properly assembled. I had already put Obie's saddle on, so that – *finally!* – there was nothing left to do but climb on and ride.

My initial impression from the saddle was that Obie was a smooth ride who needed only the lightest nudge in the ribs, and a minimal amount of rein, to do what I wanted him to. He walked around the property at a stately pace, responding quickly and easily to every command. And then, of course, he turned into a stubborn old bastard.

My mistake seems to have been in directing Obie to go inside the fence, then asking him to trot. Inside the fence was his living area. It was *supposed* to be his work area, as well (traditionally called an "arena"), but after many years of retirement, Obie seemed to have taken a proprietary interest in keeping it work-free. Every time I *tsked* him, instead of trotting, he'd give a small buck and rear, throwing in an emphatic, "*Nyee!*" in case I'd missed the point. Eventually, he stopped moving altogether and simply stood in one place, ignoring the spur-wearing irritant on his back as best he could.

At such an impasse, Connie had advised me, one should order the horse to walk backward. Horses, she insists, hate to 'back,' and when they finally do what they've been told to do, not having to back up anymore is their reward. Backing also helps to refocus their attention on you, instead of on the other horses, the dog, or the fly buzzing their ear.

But of course, such advice is only practical with horses who are *not* named Stubborn Old Bastard. Obie's response to my repeated commands to back up was to cop an attitude and take the initiative: *You want me to back up? Watch this!* At which point he proceeded to back himself all over the arena. Into the fence. Into his water bucket. Back and back and back we went until I became seriously alarmed about my lack of control. Obie refused to stop no matter how many times I tugged on the reins and hollered *Whoa!* Things were *way* out of hand. It was time to remind him who was boss.

Longeing is a thing that serves two purposes – it helps dispel a horse's excess energy, and it reminds the horse that you, the human, are in control of his immediate future. It works like this: you stand in the middle of the arena, with or without a rope attached to the horse (in Obie's case, *with* a rope). You command the horse to walk, trot, and lope, alternately, in circles around you. He must keep moving until you tell him otherwise, and I can tell *you* that when I cracked that training whip near his feet, Obie finally made the decision to do as I told him. It was a gratifying moment indeed when he acquiesced; it was his way of telling me that he would let me be in charge for a change.

After a few circles at each speed, I knew I had his attention. I put the bridle back on him and decided to explore a theory I'd been chewing on – that while he was clearly unwilling to be ridden in his living room, he *might* be willing to work outside the fence. So I rode him out on to the property. He went willingly, without any of the obstinance he'd displayed just minutes before. Halfway across the yard, I *tsked*, and to my considerable surprise, Obie broke into a trot.

As it was almost time for Sam and Farrell to leave, I only rode for a short while longer. In a brief fit of madness, Sam asked if I felt safe enough on Obie to keep riding when they left. The question ran completely counter to her overly-cautious nature: for weeks, I'd been hearing about how I could only ride when someone was home – a precaution I agreed with, actually – and now here she was suggesting that if I felt sufficiently comfortable with Obie, she and the Mr. would go ahead and leave! Some small, egotistical part of me wanted to say *sure, go ahead, I'm fine!,* but I knew better, and the fact was that I *wasn't* comfortable risking life and limb on an unpredictable horse if no one was there to call 911. So I dismounted and called it a day.

That ride on Obie – the ride I'd been hoping for, lusting after, dreaming of – left me subdued. Because he'd been so snotty in the arena, he'd taken some of the joy out of the experience. I felt underwhelmed, and very aware of the fact that I still had a lot to learn about horses. I wouldn't have minded that so much if Obie hadn't rubbed my nose in it so many times! Discouraged, I was not inclined to ride him again any time soon, but you know what they say about getting back on. And so I did, a few days later. Riding well away from the arena, Obie was a model of decorum. It was a start.

As time went on, and we learned more about each other, Obie came to trust that I was, if not an expert horsewoman, then at least *working* on it. I'm convinced that his newfound reserve of patience stemmed from the fact that our rides broke up his otherwise monotonous days of unchallenged boredom. When he and Red were in training, there were workouts to think about, and competitions to do. In retirement, there was nothing to keep his keen mind occupied. It must've been a dull existence for him.

Meanwhile, I was surprised to discover that I had my own lesson to learn with Obie. We found ourselves, one summer day, standing atop the sort of small hill upon which railroad tracks are laid. This particular set of tracks were only used by a sight-seeing train that meandered by once a day, so I had plenty of time to think about our next move.

I had stopped Obie on the tracks because the walk down that little hill was a steep one, and I was unsure how to proceed. I spent some minutes in the saddle, debating whether to dismount and lead him down the hill, or whether to stay put and urge him on very slowly. Moving too quickly, I thought, might just result in one of those unscheduled dismounts that I was keen to avoid. I was awash with indecision. A more experienced rider would've known what to do more easily than I, but then, it's exactly this sort of situation that *makes* a rider experienced.

Finally, for no other reason than pure laziness, I decided to remain in the saddle, and gave Obie the command to walk. Leaning back to balance myself, I took a deep breath and thought, *Here goes nuthin'!* Given the steepness of the hill, I was fairly certain that I'd end up pitching forward, out of the saddle and onto the ground.

To my everlasting surprise, Obie picked his way slowly down the hill. My concern had been unnecessary — he'd already figured out that extra care was needed. I had underestimated his intelligence, and I was bothered by that: you're supposed to be able to trust your mount, and it hadn't even occurred to me to give him the benefit of the doubt. Inwardly, I kicked myself for that glaring omission, and as we rode on, I made Obie a solemn promise: *I'll never make that mistake again! From here on in, I trust you, buddy!*

Froggy

(PART ONE)

Toward the end of spring, neighbor Sharon quit her job. She'd been caring for a cantankerous old woman ever since I'd moved into the chicken coop, and being treated badly on a daily basis was taking its' toll. Everyone around her breathed a sigh of relief when she finally decided that she'd had enough. Once she quit, she found herself with spare time on her hands, and I found myself with a walking partner.

Sharon will be the first to tell you that she has ADD, which can sometimes be a bit tricky to deal with. For one thing, you can tell that things don't always process in Sharon's brain the way they do in other people, so there are times when it seems like she hasn't been listening. Much to my surprise, though, when it came to exercise, that ADD came in handy: together, we walked farther, and faster, than I did by myself.

We would walk two full loops around the park across the street. Then, for a change of scenery, we'd cross the street again and do a lap around The Village, which was the next property up from our little enclave. The Village was a small, rather exclusive subdivision of tastefully designed houses and condos. There was even a mansion on the river – now divided into apartments, with a pool behind it for the use of The Village residents. Unless you had a key to its' locked gate, though, there was no way to sneak in and cool off.

There was another water feature just outside the pool gate. It was a small cement pond, in the center of which was a marble cherub holding a vase of water which poured into the pond. Impatiens and ivy were planted around the outside of the pond, and these in turn were enclosed by a brick border. This small decorative pond stood a few feet away from the cul-de-sac that marked the half-way point where we turned around and headed home.

If you peered over the shrubs that hid the pool from the road, there was a nice view of the river. Like I said, the property was, at one time, a mansion, and much of the original wrought iron railings and landscaping remained. I'd pause by the pond for a minute to take it all in before turning for home. Sharon would always walk the few steps over to the pool gate and stand there, like she was working out a way to get over the fence.

One time, when the lock was broken, that pool gate stood wide open, inviting us in. It was an awfully hot, humid morning, and we thought, *What's the worst they can do, kick us out?* We sat for some minutes at water's edge, cooling our feet in that beautiful mansion pool.

Most walks, while Sharon wrestled with the problem of the locked gate, I would stand in front of the cherub, thinking how pretty the little fountain looked, with the ring of flowers blooming around it. The pond looked to be about three feet deep, and had been painted a pleasant shade of swimming pool blue. It was at least six feet in diameter, making it a nice place for...hey!...is that a *frog* sitting there between the cherub's feet? It is! Cool! Even Sharon left her musings by the fence to come and have a look.

He was a little guy, and green like you'd expect. Just sitting there enjoying some shade on a hot summer day. Or was he? Because of the distance from the edge of the pond to the cherub, I became convinced that the frog was stuck, and needed rescuing. So I took my shoes off and waded in. My, that water was cold! The minute I got within grabbing range, though, Froggy took a giant leap and landed in the water, well away from me.

After several attempts to catch him – in which it became clear that he had the home court advantage and I was just a giant clumsy landlubber, I realized that Froggy was there by choice. I climbed back out, thoroughly refreshed, and vowed to check on him the next day, just to make sure.

Thus began a routine that continued for the rest of the summer. As we reached the cul-de-sac, Sharon would head for the pool gate, and I would check on Froggy. Sometimes, it seemed that he had already gone home for the night – somewhere in the impatiens, I imagine – for he was nowhere to be found. Other times, he'd be lying in his usual spot in the shade of the cherub.

I'd greet him fondly, "Hi Froggy! How ya doin'?" He wouldn't answer. He never did.

That little green frog became a focus for Sharon and I. Any number of times, we speculated on where he went at night, and how he had found the pond to begin with. The river bank would have been a more obvious choice, but Froggy seemed content with his fancy mansion pond. Who could blame him, really? That marble probably felt pretty good on his tummy on those ninety-degree days. However he came to be where he was, he brought a surprising amount of pleasure to our walks.

I've never been a huge fan of frogs, but I've never minded them, either. Once or twice a year, I'll spot one in the soggy greenery under the always-leaking communal spigot outside Sharon's house. During spring and summer, they're easy to spot at the park across the street: they live around the edges of the marsh there. In the still of the evenings, I can hear them croaking.

There was something different about Froggy, though, something indefinable that made him stand out as an individual. Maybe it was the fact that he'd chosen a fairly exclusive neighborhood for himself, one that Sharon or I might've chosen if we'd had the money. Maybe it was the fact that we seemed to be the only ones who knew about him. Maybe it was nothing more than our mutual fondness for all things critter. Who can say?

As the summer wound down, I began to wonder what would become of Froggy. In the wild, frogs will dig down underneath the bottom of the pond and hibernate through the winter in their mud nest. But Froggy didn't have a mud nest, unless it was under the impatiens. I posed the question to Sharon. She dismissed my concern, figuring that he was a wild animal, and would know what to do when the time came. I hoped she was right.

Unfortunately, we'll never know. As we came up on the cul-de-sac one fine September day, we noticed different things: I noticed that the caretaker had drained the pond. Sharon noticed the dead frog at the bottom of that pond. He was lying belly-up, as if he'd made one last valiant attempt to escape, and then had no more strength left to right himself when he'd failed.

It was a shocking sight. It was clear that he'd become trapped by the high walls when the water had been drained, and hadn't been able to surmount those walls. Jeez. It had only been a few days since our last walk... *how had no one noticed that there was a frog in the pond?* When the caretaker drained the thing, *how did he not notice?* We were both stunned.

My first instinct was to get Froggy's corpse out of the pond and take it home for a proper burial. Angry at all those manse-dwellers who were so busy driving around in their Jags that they couldn't be bothered to notice the frog who'd adopted them, I was damned if the poor guy was going to spend eternity there. I climbed down into the empty pond and picked him up. Ever conscious of germs, Sharon broke off two big leaves from a nearby plant and gave them to me. I wrapped Froggy in them as she cast about for a place to bury him. "Oh, no," I told her, "he's going home with us." We walked away in silence.

We were about half-way down the block before I started venting about the caretaker, the drained pond, and the oblivious neighbors. I think at one point, Sharon was on the verge of tears, and I might've been, too, but for the fact that I was busy being angry. As we walked up our driveway, I told her that I would find a good place for him out by the electronic fence, where the Witless's dogs wouldn't bother his grave. A little uncertain what the protocol for dead frogs was, Sharon broke off a sprig from her rosemary plant and set it on the leaf next to Froggy. It would be buried with him.

I went looking for a small box to put him in, but decided on some olive green tissue paper instead. The color seemed appropriate. I wrapped Froggy in it, taping the package like it was a Christmas gift. I grabbed the shovel, and an industrial-sized jar of cayenne pepper – useful for keeping the Witless's dogs away from things, and marched through the back yard.

Notfairnotfairnotfair, went the cadence in my head. It wasn't fair, and this time, it really got to me. I mean, *of course* life isn't fair. We all know that, and we all accept it, however grudgingly. But when a harmless little frog spends who-knows-how-many days struggling to get out of an empty pond before dying of thirst and hunger, because no one around him could be bothered to notice his existence, *it's just not fair!*

I dug a hole and carefully placed Froggy in it. I sprinkled a little cayenne pepper over him, covered him with dirt and more pepper, and asked the Gods to take him right up to frog heaven. With that, I stomped back across the yard, thinking that next year – if there *was* a next year at the manse pond – things would be much different. Next year, I would do what I should've done to begin with: grab a net, catch the little guy and take him to the park across the street. Why do I always think of these things too late?

Notfairnotfairnotfair.

I can't save them all. I know that. I'm prepared to concede the occasional mouse, duckling, or chipmunk. But sometimes, it's personal. Froggy was personal. I have a lot of trouble with the idea of innocents being needlessly hurt – ducks, frogs. Children. Sometime it feels like I spend a lot of energy struggling to right a distant wrong that never <u>can</u> be fixed. The shrink says I have a strong need for things to be fair. She's right. You can imagine how often life frustrates that need.

Every single night, as I lie in bed, I make a mental list of all my blessings, and I thank the Gods for them. I also make a request: "Please keep all the critters safe and healthy." Sometimes, I don't think they're listening.

Ducky

Ducky first appeared on the pond in mid-summer. He looked exactly like Pretty Boy's bespectacled brother: black feathers, white breast, white rings around his eyes. A bit skinnier than Pretty Boy, but you'd swear that they were related, nonetheless. I'll never know who dumped him, or why, but judging from the easy way he approached me during feeds, he was clearly used to being around humans. And while he integrated easily enough with the other ducks, it took me a while to warm up to him: for one thing, he was…well….*funny looking*.

Well, it's not as if I denied him food or anything. He simply struck me as a cheap imitation of my favorite duck, and I was getting frankly a little weary with the number of ducks being abandoned: the pond was averaging two dumped ducks every year. In an age when entire web sites were devoted to pleas to not dump domestic ducks in the wild, there really was no excuse for people to still be doing it.

So I fed the new guy along with all the others, but never really bothered to extend the hand of friendship to him as I had with the gang. Truth be told, the only reason I gave him a name was for storytelling purposes, because in late fall, he became a story.

I was sitting on the ground tossing corn, as usual. The ducks and I were enjoying some unseasonably mild weather, and the fact that they hadn't started getting jumpy yet added to the overall serenity. I was giving my usual commentary ("Hello, ducks! There's Lady, and Big Boy! Good morning, Freckle! And here you are, Pretty Boy! Come have corn, there's plenty for everyone!"), when I noticed a length of fishing line among all the feet. The line was moving, which meant it was caught on one of the ducks. I grasped the line and pulled gently.

I pulled a little harder, and a little harder still – not yanking, just reeling in my catch slowly and firmly. The ducks parted like the Red Sea, and there stood Ducky, attached to the line. He bent over and laid his head on the ground, and for one panic-stricken moment, I thought the line had wrapped around his neck and I was strangling him. But the line wasn't around his neck, it was down his throat: he had swallowed a fish hook. Without a moment's hesitation, I scooped him into my arms and headed for the car.

Whether it had to do with Ducky being male, or because my initial grip on him wasn't so great, I don't know, but Ducky put up one heck of a fight. I made the mistake of opening the trunk of the car right in front of him, which was stupid: experience had already taught me that ducks *really* don't like to see that trunk lid flying open. Ducky flapped his wings so wildly, I thought he might just get away, but the Gods smiled, I recovered my grip, and Ducky ended up safely in the ever-present critter carrier. I put him in the passenger seat and explained about the Avian Specialist as we made our way there.

The bird doctor wasn't in this time, either, and the task fell again to the vet who had dealt with the wild mallard I had brought in before. But the doctor was in quite a snit this morning, and during the course of the day, I ended up hearing any number of unpleasant comments from the back room about people who bring ducks in for treatment. Considering the fact that he had employed the Avian Specialist for just this purpose, I was mystified by his attitude.

The first thing that was made emphatically clear to me was that Ducky would require surgery to remove the hook. I had assumed that it would be a simple matter of pulling the hook out of the tissue in his throat, but the doctor insisted that this would be too stressful for Ducky, and that it would be best to anesthetize him. Naturally, anesthetizing him would cost money, so the second thing that was made emphatically clear to me was that they expected to be paid in full – to the tune of $165 – before they began.

I gathered from the overheard comments that Doctor thought a person would be foolish to pay the requisite sum for surgery on a duck, but what choice did I have? To ignore the problem would have been unconscionable. I endured the comments, wrote the check, and told the desk staff that I would be back for Ducky later in the day. Driving away from the office, I said a small prayer to the Gods, asking them to see Ducky safely through the operation.

I called Doctor's office around midday to check on his progress. I was told that Ducky had indeed survived the surgery and was ready to go home. When I picked him up, they showed me the hook they had removed from his throat, which had a frightening length of fishing line still attached. On the way back to the pond, Ducky made his feelings about the day known by pooping all over the inside of the carrier. I can't say that I blamed him: *I* thought Dr. Wayne was an ass, too.

I set the carrier down on the beach facing the water. The gang, whose breakfast had been interrupted by the fish hook crisis, all ran toward us enthusiastically - *at first.* Uncertain about the presence of the carrier, their run slowed to a walk, and then, as they always do when they're confused, they began to quack in consternation, turning to each other to see if any among them had the answer to this confounding puzzle: Does she have corn? Does she not have corn? *Is there corn?!*

I opened the carrier door, expecting Ducky to race out to his mates, but, in no apparent hurry, he merely walked. I was concerned that the experience with me would make him fearful of joining future feeds, but I needn't have worried. Feeling guilty about the abbreviated morning feed, I drove home, retrieved the rest of the corn, and drove back to the pond, putting paid to the question, *Is there corn?!* Clearly unwilling to hold a grudge, there was Ducky, tucking into the food just two feet away from me without a care in the world.

It was nice to know that we still had a shot at friendship.

Froggy

(PART TWO)

A few days after our discovery of the dead frog, neighbor Sharon and I took another walk around The Village. As we approached the fountain, I asked if she could see any other frogs. I was kidding, but Sharon scanned the empty pond anyway. It wasn't really empty at all, but had a complement of dead leaves scattered around the bottom. Among them she spotted a small frog. "I saw him jump," she said excitedly. Sure enough, there was our original frog.

About half-way through the summer, a large frog had appeared between the cherub's feet. Sharon swore it was a different, bigger frog, while I maintained that our original little guy had simply done some summer growing. What a surprise to find that there had indeed been two frogs all along. And this one appeared to still be alive.

I climbed down into the fountain. Expecting the frog to leap away from me, I employed a sideways-on tactic: I laid my left hand down a few feet away to distract him while my right hand swooped in and scooped him up before he could react. Once I had him in my hand, though, I realized that he was too far gone to react: he barely even moved when I picked him up. As Sharon hauled me up out of the pond, I told her I wasn't sure he would make it.

"Well, what do you want to do with him," she asked, casting about for a potential burial site.

"What I should've done to begin with. I'm gonna take him to the pond across the street and give him a proper home."

As we walked away, I expressed my concern about the frog's lack of response. Sharon, who'd studied nursing back in the day, decided that he looked dehydrated. Several times, she doused him with water from the bottle she'd brought with her, and I think the third dousing was the charm because I felt a distinct *twitch* on the palm of my hand. Even so, there was little reason for hope: apart from that one twitch, he didn't move, didn't try to escape, didn't even seem to be conscious. Grimly, I hoped for the best, and prepared for the worst.

When we reached the park, we walked up and down the boardwalk that borders the pond, searching for new home sites. I wanted a patch of mud, I told Sharon, because I didn't think he was ready to be tossed into the water just yet, and I didn't want a drowned frog on my conscience. I settled uneasily for a mud patch just off the boardwalk where it intersects the path coming in from the street. It was a busy area, and I'd seen dogs and kids in the vicinity of where I now set the frog, but it was the only mud patch I'd seen on a pond full of cattails and reeds, so it would have to do.

The little guy considered the mud briefly before throwing himself into the water. Once there, he seemed to hang, suspended, between the bottom of the pond, and the surface. Crouching at water's edge, I looked up at Sharon. "Did he just commit frog suicide?"

"No," she said impatiently, "he's exchanging CO_2 for oxygen. It's what they do."

"And you know this about frogs because why?"

"Because we studied biology in nursing school."

Well, I hadn't even studied biology in high school – and it was a required course! Who was I to argue? I only hoped she was right.

I took a second walk in the park by myself, later that same day. I wanted to check on the little frog's progress. I was dissatisfied with the location of his new home, and worried that I would be responsible for hastening his untimely demise. It took me one loop around the park trail to conclude that he should be moved – the sooner the better.

One of the reasons I wanted to move him was that I'd passed a woman on the trail who had with her a strangely frenetic child – almost a cross between autism and hyperactivity, and he'd been pottering about in uncomfortable proximity to the little frog's mud patch. But that wasn't the only thing.

A year or so ago, while I'd been walking at the park, I had come upon a woman with three small dogs on leashes. I'd seen her around before. More than once, she'd allowed them to wander off the trail. Never mind all the signs saying *Please keep all activity on the path,* or the fact that this was a nature preserve, designed to maintain a protective environment for any number of woodland creatures – no, what seemed to matter to that woman was letting her three dogs do whatever they wanted, wherever they wanted to do it. And that day, a year or so ago, one of them wanted to chew on a big frog he'd found. When I happened on the scene, it looked like the frog was still alive.

"Aren't you going to do anything," I'd asked, "it looks like he's still alive." She responded by saying that she was certain the frog was dead.

"But he's still moving," I pointed out.

"Not really, it's just a reflexive thing."

"Well, *I'll* get the poor frog out of his mouth!"

"I wouldn't, Hector might bite you."

I walked away then, disgusted by her obvious disinterest in that poor frog's needless death. All the while, Hector continued to chew on the corpse. It had been a disturbing encounter: this stupid woman regularly brought her dogs to a *nature preserve* for exercise, without, it seemed, giving any thought to what the place was about. The incident left me sad and angry.

So I ratted her out to Ernie the park ranger. I spent so much time at the park over the years that Ernie knew me on sight. We'd had any number of chats about the preserve and its critter residents, and I learned enough about him to see that he had a certain fondness for the place. I told him I figured that the frog had more right to be there than some ditz who chose not to control her dogs, and he agreed. He promised to keep an eye out for her, and bring her up to speed on park rules.

It was that woman and her frog-chewing dogs I worried about as I considered finding a safer location for my amphibian friend. When I peered down under the boardwalk, I saw that he'd left the water and was now happily sunning himself on the mud patch. Assuming that he was feeling rejuvenated – and therefore more able to evade me, I used a stealth approach. Using the tall grass for cover, I sneaked in as close as possible, then moved swiftly, closing my hand around him so fast he didn't even realize he'd been captured again until he was safely in my hand.

I greeted him softly, knowing that once I found a better spot away from the boardwalk, I'd probably never see him again. I was o.k. with that, as long as it meant he was safe. I wandered over to the reeds and cattails. Inspecting them closely, I saw there was plenty of mud for him, and plenty of cover, as well. We were far enough away from the boardwalk that he'd be protected from frenetic children and marauding dogs. Here, I thought, was a good home for a frog, and with that, I set him down on a patch of mud. He considered the mud briefly, then jumped into the water and swam away.

Feeling pleased and relieved, and heading toward home, I looked up to see that the ditz with the frog-chewing dogs just happened to be headed my way. What timing! Knowing that those merciless little ankle-biters would soon be walking right past where Froggy had been just moments before made me shake my head in wonder: *sometimes, the Gods just hand you one on a silver platter, don't they?!*

I know that frog rescues must seem silly to most people, but here's the thing: what if, when you get to the pearly gates, what if the Gods ask you about *that one frog*? What if they want to know about the one critter you couldn't be bothered with because you were late for a meeting, and he was probably already dead anyway? What if that's the one and only question they have for you – *why didn't you help?*

Time Out

There came a time when the mantle of responsibility began to weigh heavily on me. The final straw came when I was walking at the park across the street, and found a female mallard floating belly-up in the pond. Her five ducklings – half-grown but still too young to fly – paddled about a few yards away, peeping the unanswerable question, *where'd you go, mama?* I have no idea how she died.

The image of that poor dead duck floating in the water stayed with me, and I took that mental picture to my therapist, shedding tears of despair on the way to her office. *I'm so tired,* I told her. Depression does that to you. It saps you of your energy, making you want to go back to bed and sleep for a few years.

I didn't *mind* my obligations. In fact, feeding the gang at McKinnon's Pond was the high point of my mornings: as spring progressed, more and more wild mallards turned up for feeds with ducklings in tow. Even a couple of domestics had managed babies, in spite of Officer Dave's thoroughness. By mid-summer, McKinnon's Pond was teeming with ducks, and my spirits soared.

But a series of unrelated events – all small but irritating reminders of my complete lack of control in the universe, brought my lengthy spell of relative peace to an end. The discovery of the duck corpse threw me off kilter. Depression began to build, and I knew it was time to get out of Dodge for a while.

When you are a Crazy Critter Lady, going away for any length of time is no easy proposition. There are not only the cats to consider, but a pond-full of ducks, as well. While I'm not quite as nutty as Sharon – who leaves the t.v. turned to Animal Planet for her cats when she goes to work, I *am* unwilling to put my cats through any undue stress. Boarding them is out of the question, if for no other reason than *I* wouldn't want to spend a week cooped up in a cage. And reliable sitters are hard to find.

I found out too late that the last professional sitter I hired liked looking after cats because she thought she didn't have to do anything more than give them food and scoop a little poop. By the time I got home from that trip, poor Buddy – half-feral, *don't touch me!*, Buddy – was frantic with loneliness, and followed me all over the chicken coop for days. All the cats suffered from that sitter's careless disregard, and I vowed that next time would be different.

Rummaging through the Yellow Pages, a small ad caught my eye: "We Specialize In Cats!" There was a bit of phone tag involved before I finally got a live person on the line – apparently, the Cat Lady was in demand. Diane seemed genuinely happy with her chosen profession, figuring it was merely an extension of her home life. At one point in time, she and her husband had owned *twenty cats!* This was my kind of woman! Well-versed in basic medical procedures like insulin injections and sub-cutaneous fluid treatments, I felt confident that she'd be able to give Buddy his daily pill.

What sold me on Diane was her approach to scaredy cats. If they hid under the bed during her visit, she would bring a book, sit on the bedroom floor, and read a few chapters. This would have been my approach exactly: be present without being intrusive, and I knew Buddy would be comforted by it. In the meantime, I could begin planning my trip with an easier mind.

During previous travels, I had missed the cats dreadfully, feeling guilty because I knew they didn't understand my absence. There were even times when I seriously considered cutting trips short and coming home early. This time, though, with the right sitter at the helm, I felt sure I could get through a week in London with only a few small twinges of homesickness.

I intended to take a few riding lessons in Hyde Park, an idea that amused me no end: even on vacation, I'd be spending time with critters! And, if I felt the need to commune with water fowl, I knew I could find them in abundance at St. James's Park.

I had passed a pleasant couple of hours in St. James's Park on a previous trip. Almost out of money, and casting about for cheap ways to amuse myself, I'd stumbled into the park by accident.

Tucked behind the massive stone buildings of Whitehall lies a surprising oasis of tranquility. I clearly wasn't the only one who thought so. On that sunny afternoon, old folks and young couples alike availed themselves of the park benches that London has in commendable abundance. Like me at McKinnon's Pond, some of these people were obvious regulars, bringing with them sacks of bread for the ducks. But while there were numerous breeds of ducks in the park, there were, alas, no Pekins. Which just goes to show you that even royalty has its faults, for it's the Queen who owns that little slice of heaven.

In any case, Diane kindly agreed to look after the ducks as well, which was a huge relief. I knew that other people fed them, I just didn't know how often, or whether it was nutritious. So I stocked up on cracked corn, piling the bags onto the back seat of my car. All Diane had to do was grab a bag and go. Knowing that the gang would continue to receive healthy food in my absence cleared the last hurdle before the trip: now I could pack up my suitcase and go.

According to its' website, Heathrow Airport serves over sixty-seven *million* passengers a year, making it the third largest airport in the world. Employing over sixty-eight thousand people, Heathrow generates five billion pounds sterling for the local economy. On any given day, thousands of people pass through its' terminals, carrying God only knows how much luggage. In spite of these impressive facts, though, I had no trouble spotting my suitcase on the carousel: it was the one covered in cat hair.

I had brought the thing down from the attic a couple of weeks before the trip, and set it in a corner of the bedroom. Gracie immediately took possession, and really only left it to eat or use the litter box. The other cats began to wonder what was so special about the big box that Gracie wanted it all to herself, and Buddy and Junebug both gave it test-naps in her absence. It ended up looking like a giant fuzzball on wheels, and since I didn't care enough to break out the lint roller, the cat hair remained. Once in London, the giant fuzzball was a happy reminder of what waited for me at the end of my trip.

On day two my vacation, I set off in happy anticipation of my first English riding lesson. Unfortunately, while the lesson was interesting, it left me feeling like something was missing. And indeed it was: in the States, the grooming and hoof-picking gave me time to bond with Crazy, and it gave her time to get to know me. Was I gentle? Did I seem to know what I was doing? Did I treat her with respect? These questions were all answered by my tone of voice, and my touch, and Crazy responded accordingly. In turn, by taking the time to talk to her, and familiarize myself with her personality, I came to know Crazy as the gentle, amiable old horse that she is.

By contrast, at the London stable where I met up with my instructors, there was none of this bonding business. I was simply handed a horse, already tacked up, and told to get on. And while my US instructor had repeatedly told me to go into these English lessons with an open mind, the lack of socializing time with the horses bothered me. When the same thing happened at the second lesson, instead of getting on the horse, I stood my ground and asked if he had a name. I was told it was Monty. I said hello and gave him a friendly pat, and that was the sum total of my interaction with the horses for any of my lessons.

So while it was indeed quite something to trot through Hyde Park on a horse the size of a small building (the stable seemed to have a fondness for huge horses), there was also something very impersonal about the way it was done. I had looked forward to making some critter friends in London – no matter that our friendships would be brief – but it became clear by the end of my first lesson that that wasn't going to happen.

I knew that I wouldn't be making any duck friends at St. James's Park, either, but I went anyway. I walked all the way around the pond and never once picked up on any discernable duck personalities. Perhaps it's only Pekins who have character. Perhaps it's the same difference as dogs and wolves – domestic animals and wild – the tame critters wanting to be part of things, and the wild ones wanting no part of humanity at all. Either way, my London critter interactions were not going according to plan.

There are, of course, plenty of other diversions besides animals to avail yourself of in London. Shopping there is practically an Olympic sport in its' own right. With everything from Harrods, to department and specialty stores, to antique and street markets, there truly is something for everyone. I myself am not a good shopper – I tend to wear out quickly and become cranky and bitchy, but I gave it a good try anyway.

One of the things I bought gave me pause for thought in the store. It was a powder blue down coat with a faux fur hood that was so obviously faux, I felt comfortable buying it. But the hood wasn't the problem.

The problem was that the down contained within was not the usual goose down – which I wouldn't have minded because the geese at the pond are so mean to my gang – but rather, duck down. Uh-oh.

It may surprise you to learn that I am not a vegetarian. Not even close. I'm a carnivore, albeit a fairly picky one. I was once invited to drinks at Lord and Lady Witless's. After an hour or so of wine and chat, I got up to leave. The Witlesses extended an invitation to stay for dinner, and to sweeten the offer, they said enticingly, "We're having *duck*!" My response was a Phoebe Buffay-style, "I couldn't possibly, I have friends who are ducks!" So while I do eat meat, I make it a policy not to eat any specie that I've enjoyed a first-name relationship with, which made the decision whether to buy a coat filled with duck down all the more contentious.

I know what you're thinking: *But she already has a down coat – the one with the feathers of thousand geese in it. Why buy another?* The easy answer is that I'm a girl, and girls can never have too many of anything. So I bit my lip, asked a small prayer of forgiveness from the Gods, and bought the coat. I will not be wearing it when I go to feed the gang in winter.

I managed to stuff the new coat into my suitcase for the return journey. It took up an awful lot of space. I always pack an extra, collapsible bag to hold my purchases, but I invariably buy a whole lot more than one collapsible bag can hold. Several years ago, I learned that I could save myself the agony of dragging a much-too-heavy suitcase through the world's third-largest airport by mailing things home. The only caveat: you're not supposed to mail stuff to yourself. Not wishing to impose on the goodwill of my neighbors, I sent several boxes in care of Muffi, June, and Grace Meister. The antique cricket bat was mailed in care of Buddy.

In the meantime, the day before I departed for London, Crazy Crocodile Guy Steve Irwin was killed by a stingray off the coast of Australia. Irwin was a bit too *out there* even for my tastes, but it must be said that he really did die doing what he loved. Unfortunately, toward the end of my vacation, London newspapers reported that stingrays were being slaughtered by angry Aussies in some twisted attempt to avenge Irwin's death.

This was crushing news, and the singular irony was that I don't for a minute believe that Irwin would have approved of the wholesale massacre of creatures that he loved and respected. The harsh reality of mans' inhumanity to nature had followed me across an ocean, and it cast a pall over my trip. No matter how many stories of animal cruelty I hear, I never cease to be horrified and depressed by them.

Thankfully, my own critters were being well looked-after. Owing to a preponderance of internet cafes all around the capitol, I was able to keep my emails up to date. I received one from neighbor Sharon, saying that she'd seen Diane coming and going twice a day. She claimed that Diane always had a contented look on her face as she drove off.

In the interest of keeping homesickness at bay, I deliberately avoided thinking about the cats and ducks waiting for me back in the States. I managed this fairly well most of the time. At night, though, lying in my hotel bed, I would pause in my review of the day long enough to ask the Gods to take good care of my guys. Half-way through the trip, I began to anticipate going home: the hotel bed was much too big without five cats to keep me company, and St. James's Park was much too quiet without a gang of sociable ducks quacking up a storm.

There had been many years when London was a happy escape for me. Escape from the crack addict, escape from myself and my miserable existence. For six or seven stolen days – days I could ill afford but for the credit cards that I would later file bankruptcy on – I was safe, content, at peace. Those were joyous trips for me, filled with wonder at a new and interesting culture. Every day was an adventure, and I relished the challenges of keeping myself fed, crossing the streets safely, and getting where I wanted to go on a foreign transport system. It was terrific fun.

But now, after fifteen-plus years of therapy, I found that I didn't need the escape like I used to. It came as quite a surprise to find myself in my favorite city, wanting nothing more than to be back in my drafty chicken coop with my five feline pals, and photos of ducks and horses taking up every available bit of space. I still love London, but I no longer feel a pressing need to be there – especially when I know I'm wanted back home.

And so it was that after three security checks, a head to toe x-ray scan, a full body pat-down by a large, unpleasant-looking woman who should be named Helga, three hours of time-killing in the duty-free shops, over seven hours of flying time, *and* an hour's ride home from the airport, I dragged my still-too-heavy luggage inside the chicken coop door and....nothing. Not one cat came out to greet me.

I went looking, of course, just to make sure they were still there. I found Spanky under the bed, staring out at me with big reproachful eyes that said, *who are you, and where have you been?* It took him ten minutes to decide to come out and greet me. In the meantime, I moved on to the living room, where I found Gracie, Muffin and Junebug, all lounging about with that *oh, have you been gone?* expression on their faces. Buddy wandered in, not looking the least bit traumatized, as I had expected. Apparently, Diane had taken *very* good care of them.

According to the notes she kept, every single cat behaved differently than I had predicted. I expected Muffin to be the most affable, when in fact she spent the week under the kitchen table being crabby and bitchy. I expected Junebug to be sociable, but she spent the week in her favorite basket above the refrigerator. I expected Gracie to hide when Diane came, but she turned out to be the friendliest one of all, running to greet Diane at every visit.

Because I had expected Buddy to suffer his usual semi-feral pangs of loneliness for the one human he felt close to, I was very surprised to read that not only had he let Diane give him his daily pill, but he let her *pet him*, as well. This was an extraordinary turn of events.

The day she came to give him a practice pill, before the trip, he managed to evade her every attempt and in fact, she never got near enough to try. It had been a concern to both of us, and I had given her back-up phone numbers – Sam's was one of them – of people I thought could manage Buddy's pill if she couldn't. And yet now, I read that he'd developed a routine of hiding under the bedspread, and allowing Diane to uncover him long enough for a pill. Then she'd cover him back up, pet him over the bedspread, and tell him what a wonderful boy he was. She wasn't wrong.

It was Spanky – gentle, delicate Spanky – who appeared to have suffered from my absence. Sometimes I forget what a fragile nature he has, for in her notes, Diane remarked that Spanky never once came out to eat while she was there; he remained under the bed, exactly as I found him when I returned. I'm sure that he ate after she left, but the fact that he wanted no part of interaction with her – or indeed with anyone else, saddens me. Spanky appears to be a one-person cat, which must have been very lonely for him while I was gone.

The ducks, on the other hand, didn't seem to realize that I *had* been gone. When I showed up for a feed the day after my return, they all gathered around, quacking as if they'd just seen me the day before. As always, I was cheered by their enthusiasm – it was a marked contrast to the ho-hum reception I'd gotten from the cats.

The ducks seem to have charmed Diane, as well, for she wrote a separate page about them, remarking on how much she'd enjoyed getting to know them. And here's the kicker: claiming that McKinnon's Pond was on the way to her next sitting job, Diane told me there was no need to pay her extra for feeding them. My suspicion is that that garrulous gang of domestics wormed their way into her heart just as they had mine.

It was good to be home. I had enjoyed London well enough, shopping and horseback riding and searching out adventure as I'd done. It's a nice feeling to be at large in a big city, with relatively few responsibilities, and no one to answer to. But I find that *purpose* is a big theme in life, especially when you struggle with issues of depression and low self-esteem. It's important to have a reason to get out of bed in the mornings, and in London, I did not.

Back in the States, in the town I call home, there *are* reasons to get out of bed: because the cats wouldn't let me stay there for very long anyway, and because those ducks aren't going to feed themselves. It may seem silly to you, but to me, they're all family – a *chosen* family that will never hurt me, never turn a blind eye, never lie. They love me no matter what I look like, or what kind of mood I'm in. You can't ask much more than that.

A few days after I returned from London, Junebug and I enjoyed a nuzzle on the kitchen floor.

I missed you the most, Kelly!
I missed <u>you</u> the most, Little Mitten!

Changes

There were a couple of changes in the months after my trip to London. First, I decided to volunteer out at the barn where I took riding lessons. The more riding lessons I took, the more I needed and wanted to spend time with horses. I approached Nancy, the owner, and offered to trade barn work for knowledge: *teach me what you know about horses, and I'll happily scoop poop for you!* She told me to come out on Saturday mornings, and I've been going ever since.

Saturdays aren't about riding – something I rarely get to do then, anyway. Every once in a while, as a thank-you for all the free labor, Nancy will offer to let me spend some time on Ruckus, who replaced Crazy as my lesson horse. It's a nice perk, but neither necessary nor expected. Mostly, I'm interested in learning horse anatomy, horse illness and injury, horse behavior. Horse *everything!*

Helping on Saturdays has been much more than a learning experience; it's been one of those altruistic things that gives me a day-long buzz: every week, I have tangible proof that I have done a good thing for someone other than myself. It shows in the clean water buckets and stalls. It shows in the horses that know me now, and respond with affection and respect. And it shows in one feisty donkey who brays when she sees me coming up the driveway. It's a whole critter family out there, and they have welcomed me with open arms.

The other change involved moving out of the chicken coop. This was not initially of my choosing, but rather, because Lord Witless informed me that they'd need the place for his mother-in-law. Of all the buildings on the property, the chicken coop is the only single-floor unit; all the others have stairs. Evidently, mom-in-law was getting on in years, and the Witlesses felt the time had come to take her in.

The time had apparently come for *all* the tenants. Jack and Sharon moved out that summer, leaving behind an astounding amount of junk-furniture in the Witless's garage, and some ill-will to boot. Theirs had not been a particularly cordial relationship with Lord and Lady. The only reason mine had been so was because I was pretty good at faking it. In truth, I had no respect for the Witlesses, and once I'd made up my mind to go, I couldn't wait to get away: I'd been holding in a lot of resentment over their critter carelessness for quite some time.

Lord Witless once remarked to me how tenants always seemed to end up hating him and his wife. He said it in a puzzled tone of voice which indicated that he had no idea why anyone could *possibly* dislike him. I'll tell you why: because he and Lady W. have spent an inordinate amount of time frantically trying to climb the social ladder – with limited success – alienating in the process anyone whom they deemed to be "not of our social class." They're the biggest snobs I know, with the least amount of reason to be that way, and it's frankly tacky and gross.

To be fair, the Witlesses *did* originally offer me the apartment above the garage, but there wasn't much point in this if I wanted to get away from them, so I started looking first at apartments, and then at houses. The apartments were all heartbreakingly small and depressing: little or no room for storage, and even less room for five cats to stretch out and be comfortable. Yes, the cats were actually my main consideration: if they were happy, then so was I. If they were unhappy, I would be deeply so.

Looking at houses in my price range was equally depressing. They were, to the last, postage-sized dumps in neighborhoods I didn't want to live in anyway. Things were going from bad to worse, and there were still the ducks to consider! That's right, the ducks were second on my list of priorities. The house had to be big enough for the cats, roomy enough for my stuff, and not too far away from the pond. It was beginning to look like an impossible dream.

I've learned to embrace my weirdness to a large degree. So it was with no embarrassment at all that I would announce to the realtor, "Nope, too far away from my ducks," or, "The cats would hate this!" To her credit, and because I seem to attract critter types, my realtor –

a fun young woman named Sandy – never made a disparaging comment.

The reason became clear when she told me the story of her million-dollar Weimeraner, a dog who required so much costly medical care that she refused to give him up or euthanize him on principle alone. In addition, Sandy harbored her own loner dream of owning a house located in the middle of forty acres. "With bushy trees planted all around the perimeter," I agreed dryly.

When we walked around the half-acre property in the next town over, I knew from the landscaping alone that the place was paradise. Eons ago, someone with a plan had owned that property. You could see it in the nearly-buried-now brick edging surrounding the flora. Blooming trees and shrubs had been planted all over the place, by a loving eye who knew what they'd look like when they matured. Being a gardener myself, I was immediately intrigued.

The inside of the house was roomy, in places. The two-bedroom ranch had been added on to, over the years. It was big enough now that five cats could each find their own quiet spot to nap, with plenty of windows for bird-watching. And, it was close enough to the pond that the daily commute wouldn't annoy me too much.

The price was a bit more than I was comfortable with, but I knew that that beautifully landscaped yard, with its' requisite maintenance, would keep me happily occupied for years to come, and, for once, I would be my own landlord. No more Witlesses, no more thirsty, neglected dogs, no more fate being decided by someone's mother-in-law. I was happy, and so was my shrink: her little basket case was finally growing up!

The transition from chicken coop to critter shack (as I dubbed the new place) would not be an easy one. In the midst of planning, packing and arranging – not to mention copious amounts of paperwork with the loan officer – Pretty Boy developed a problem. His right wing began to dangle down at his side. I would watch him hoist it back into position, only to see it fall back down where it had been flopping a moment before. Knowing nothing about duck anatomy, save what I can see from the outside, I was mystified. Another fish hook injury? There was only one way to find out: get him to a vet.

I called Officer Dave, asking would he please talk to the local animal hospital and see if their non-practicing Avian Specialist (who still worked on cats and dogs) would make an exception on Dave's behalf. He did, and, thank goodness, she would.

After a thorough exam, Dr. Crys decided that Pretty Boy had an abscess in his wing – and quite a large one at that. She gave him a shot of antibiotic, then put him on a two-week regimen that would grow to include a daily children's Flintstones vitamin when the antibiotics caused side-effects. Everyone who met him at the clinic was thoroughly charmed by Pretty Boy, who treated the adventure with a surprising amount of aplomb, considering the fact that he'd never once in his life left the pond.

I administered his meds faithfully every day for two weeks, hiding the ground-up pills in chunks of bread that Pretty Boy happily gobbled, but there was no change. After a consultation, Dr. Crys ordered two more weeks of antibiotics. Half-way through that second round, it was clear that Pretty Boy wasn't responding. I took him back to the clinic.

Dr. Crys took an x-ray this time. She tried to prepare me for the worst by saying that she thought Pretty Boy had a systemic infection – a thing which is, apparently, very dicey and difficult to treat. One look at the x-ray told her otherwise, though, and she came back into the exam room announcing, "I have good news and bad news."

The bad news was that Pretty Boy had a cancerous tumor in his wing that had already entirely eaten away his wrist joint. The good news was that it would be a lot easier to treat than a systemic infection. Because he was in pain, Dr. Crys insisted on one of two options: amputate half his wing, or euthanize him.

Given that domestic ducks can live over twenty years, and that Pretty Boy was only five, there was no question as to the right course of action. "Amputate," I said firmly, "he's too young to euthanize." And with that, I headed home, saying yet another in an endless string of prayers to the Gods that they take good care of this special duck, and get him through the operation. As luck would have it, they saw things my way.

I went to visit him the day after his surgery. I brought my camera with me. I had already written a short piece on Pretty Boy's condition for the local paper. It was actually a plea for funds to help cover the cost of his care, but there was an ulterior motive, as well. In my mind, the more popular the ducks became with the city's residents, the harder it would be for city administrators to try to remove them from the pond again. When I dropped off the piece to the editor, she suggested I bring her a picture of Pretty Boy at the hospital to accompany the article.

I was excited to see him walking around the large sink that they were in the process of filling for him. I was told that there had been a bandage on his wound but, not caring for the accessory, Pretty Boy had removed it. This didn't seem to be a problem. In fact, as I approached, it was clear that he was already back to his feisty old self, splashing and quacking and poking the detritus at sink's edge with his bill.

I asked one of the techs if she would take a few pictures of Pretty Boy and I, and as soon as she began snapping away, a funny thing happened: six vet techs, who had been standing around fawning over the only duck most of them had ever handled, suddenly remembered that they all owned cell phones that could take pictures. After smiling for my camera, I looked around to see six phones pointed in our direction! It was clear that they were all completely smitten with Pretty Boy.

I was all for leaving him at the hospital over the weekend. I didn't like the idea of him being vulnerable down at the pond. Who knew whether the other ducks would sense his weakness and pick on him, not to mention the usual suspects: raccoons, and the neighborhood cats and dogs. It was Dr. Crys who convinced me that he needed to get back to what she called his "home water," that place where he lived and ate and preened. Indeed, his feathers looked shockingly ratty. He'd barely done any preening at the clinic, and it showed. I saw her point, and reluctantly returned him to the pond just two days after his surgery.

He was thrilled to be back. He dashed back and forth in the shallows, quacking and paddling like he couldn't believe his good luck. I swear he was laughing, and from the shore, I was, too. It soon became apparent, though, how big a problem neglecting his preening was.

As Pretty Boy attempted to swim across the pond, his body – no longer buoyant from the lack of grooming – began to sink. Not entirely, but enough of him was under water that I became seriously alarmed and made a frantic call to the hospital. Too late: it was five minutes past closing. There was nothing for it but to make sure he got across the pond. If I had to go in after him, I would.

Thankfully, it didn't come to that, but I can tell you, it was one scary swim. As I watched, his entire body sank beneath the surface, until only his head and neck were above water. It must have been an excruciating effort to get all the way across. Once he made it to the other side, he climbed out and began to preen.

I walked over to where he was and sat down a few feet away, watching, for over an hour. It was going to take a lot longer than that to fix the problem because every last feather on that poor duck's body needed grooming. It would no doubt be an exhausting couple of days for him.

Each day after that, he looked much better. It took about three days to get all of his feathers right again. The balance problem took longer. Pretty Boy would frequently approach a feed and lose his balance, falling helplessly onto his side before struggling to right himself. It was a disturbing sight.

It never occurred to me that bird wings affect balance – even in flightless ducks – but apparently, they do. I was reluctant to pick Pretty Boy up and take him back to the hospital for his one-week follow-up, but I knew it was necessary – especially in light of his balance issue. Apologizing, I scooped him back into the carrier, and posed the question to Dr. Crys. She nodded and told me he'd work it out in a month or so.

In fact, because of the way Dr. Crys had operated, in a months' time you couldn't even tell he was missing half a wing. Wing feathers that she'd pulled for the surgery grew back, covering over what wasn't there anymore. To the untrained eye, he looked no different than he had before. Personality-wise, he was the same goofy character, shouldering his way to the front of the pack at feeding time and looking me straight in the eye as he stood in the middle of the pile of corn. It was good to know that he wasn't holding a grudge.

The cancerous wing would not be Pretty Boy's only health issue. Some months later, he managed to tear his eyelid. His new vet, Dr. Susan, stitched him up and advised that he should take it easy for a week or so. Instead of following her advice, I sent Pretty Boy back to the pond, where he promptly pulled the stitches loose. After Dr. Susan sewed him up a second time, I took him home and installed him in my bathroom.

I had no idea how often a duck poops until I found out the hard way. It seemed to be every twelve minutes! I took to laying sheets of painter's plastic drop cloth on the floor and taping it half-way up the walls: not only could Pretty Boy poop prolifically, but he could fling it across the room, as well.

I was to administer antibiotic eye drops twice a day. No matter how benevolent my intentions, Pretty Boy fought me every single time. Even when I had him pinned, more or less, in his carrier, he still managed to wiggle around enough to bite any part of me within range. He talked the whole time, too, making throaty, glottal sounds that I took to mean, "Will you *please* unhand me!" While he seemed to place a measure of trust in me, Pretty Boy was clearly determined not to go down without a fight.

He ended up enduring recurring eye infections, and spent a week in my bathroom on three separate occasions. While I'm sure that Pretty Boy thought it was the end of the world, I can assure you that *I* was the one who suffered! In the first place, duck poop really smells, and the scent of it would seep out underneath the bathroom door and waft through the living room. After a few days, it began to seem like the smell had taken up residence in the walls.

The bathtub was an issue. I made sure that Pretty Boy got tub time at least three times a day. This involved putting him in a tub-full of cold water, tossing in some cat kibbles for him to play with, and leaving him there for thirty minutes or so. Pretty Boy would make use of the time to splash and preen, and, naturally, poop, as well. By the time I cleaned the tub at the end of the day, the water was positively *green*.

Although Pretty Boy was clearly unhappy about his incarceration, he took a proprietary interest in the bathroom anyway. It soon became obvious that he considered it his own space, and let it be known that he didn't appreciate my coming in to use the toilet. He would pace back and forth by the tub, muttering those universal *duck duck duck* noises that all ducks make and letting me know that he didn't appreciate my presence in *his* room.

After each of these exhausting adventures, I would drive Pretty Boy back to the pond, wondering whether his girlfriend would remember him, and he, her. Each reunion confirmed anew for me that while they *seem* like simple creatures, those ducks actually have a lot going on upstairs. I would open the carrier door and let Pretty Boy out on the beach. He would immediately make his way to the water, splash about in the shallows and quack to Girlfriend Duck, who would come racing toward him, quacking what was clearly a greeting in return. They were always thrilled to see each other again.

It was after one of his stays in my tub that I inadvertently discovered something very touching about Pretty Boy. During my annual Planned Duckhood effort, I'd been out at the pond exchanging domestic duck eggs for store-bought chicken eggs. The girls would usually jump off their nests and hover nearby while I worked, but Freckle Duck refused to be cowed and put up quite a fight. When I picked her up, she bit hell out of my hand. Surprised by the intensity of her attack, I plopped her on the ground and inspected my index finger: sure enough, that knuckle was bleeding. It was then I realized that all this time, Pretty Boy had been pulling his punches.

I can't tell you exactly how many times he's bitten me, while in my care. Every single time I picked him up – to put him in the tub, to take him out of the tub, to put him in his carrier for eye drops, to take him out of the carrier afterward, etc. – he'd managed to wrap his bill around my flesh. But never once had it hurt the way Freckle Duck's bite had, and he'd certainly never drawn blood. It warmed my heart to learn that he cared enough about me to ensure that he didn't hurt me.

We had come a long way since his days as one of Missy's cute little ducklings. *I* had come a long way, from those early days when I merely showed up with a Zip-loc bag full of cracked corn and sat on a bench by the water. Those ducks had charmed me, all right, but they'd done much more than that. They had been the catalysts for an incredible amount of healing and change. Change is something I usually resist, which is ironic, since therapy is about nothing *but* change. But the critters had made the transitions easy. Well, eas*ier*.

When I'd first met the ducks, I was living in a tiny little apartment, depression running rampant, my life going nowhere. The ducks were a form of therapy, like the shrink, only better: the shrink had an *agenda,* the ducks just had time, patience, and love. I could leave the shrink's office in tears over some impossibility, head down to the pond, lose myself in the moment and feel much better.

Over time, those moments started adding up to months and years and a whole lot more commitment than I'd ever experienced before. Where there had been two cats, now there were five. Where there had been three ducks, now there were twelve, with an advocate who spent her own meager funds creating a poster ("I'm a *Luckey* duck, thanks to your generous donation of cracked corn to the Luckey [Inc.] Duck Fund!") that found its way all over town. Every business I approached was willing to put that poster in their window. The folks at my bank actually handed me a roll of tape and told me to pick a good spot!

Donations to the Luckey Duck Fund were generous. Indeed, Fred, my car hero down at the local garage, phoned after reading one of my duck pieces in the paper and told me to call him any time I needed corn. "If you're willing to go out and feed them every day, I'm willing to pay for it," he said. There were donations for Pretty Boy's medical expenses as well, proving that not only did people care, but that I with my writing had the power to move them to action. It was a heady time.

I'm still solidly a loner; I no longer want to be bothered with other people's dysfunction. If you're not willing to do some therapy to fix your problems, then *learn to live with your miserable self and quit bitching!* I choose my friends carefully, and keep the numbers small. Life is short, and I don't want to waste any more of it on someone else's rage, low self-esteem, or doormat tendencies. I've had enough of my own.

The child molester took far too many years away from me, years that I can never have again. That fact causes me an enormous amount of despair and depression. The good news is that slowly, over time, with the help of lots of therapy and lots of ducks and cats and horses, slowly, life is coming together in the manner that it should.

Thanks to the critters, I am becoming who I was meant to be: an animal lover, and an animal advocate. I get my needs met by caring for the animals, and they get their needs met by letting me care for them. It's a mutually agreeable arrangement that suits everyone involved.

And, I will leave behind a far better legacy than either of my parents: as a person of honesty and integrity, who refused to shrink from the truth no matter how unpalatable it was. And as a not-so-crazy Critter Lady, who could be counted on to look after the animals no one else wanted.

The critters saved me. Saved me from spending too much time alone and brooding. Saved me from feeling unloved and unworthy. No matter how little I thought of myself, animals accepted me without question. Their gift of unconditional love was a rare gem I'd never seen the like of before. Caring for them gave me a sense of purpose and accomplishment – two things I desperately needed.

And, they gave me companionship. When humans became intolerable, I could always count on the critters to extend the paw of friendship. All they asked from me was food and love. It was a small price to pay for what I got in return.

Epilogue

I've read that Krishnamurti believed that to best comfort one who is dying, we must tell him that a part of us will die along with him – thus assuring him that he will not be alone on his journey. When I first read Krishna's words, at my kitchen table, my eyes drifted to the refrigerator, where several gaily-colored magnets hold up various bits of noteworthy news. They are magnets that Winkie helped me make.

Because of the abuse I suffered as I child, I have endured a lifetime of depression. During a particularly oppressive bout a few years ago, I holed up inside my home for several weeks. I had with me a substantial lump of clay that I misappropriated from a local pottery studio. I don't know how the idea came to me, but I found myself rolling out flat slabs of clay, then pressing Winkie's paws into them over and over again, making numerous imprints of his feet.

The project continued with cutting half-dollar-sized circles around the imprints, painting the dried pieces with brightly-colored underglazes, then smuggling them all back to the studio to be fired as if I'd actually done the work there as I was supposed to. Some pieces even had claw imprints, as well. When the firing process was complete, I glued small magnets to the back of each piece. I produced so many magnets in those dark weeks that I gave a number of them to Sam and the others at Dr. Green's office. From a vantage point at Sam's dining table, I can see one of Winkie's paws securing a picture to her fridge.

I have known cats who would have found having their paws thrust into wet clay distasteful, but Winkie was not among them. He seemed to regard the adventure with the same sort of indulgence with which I let him lead our walks. He could not have known that shortly after that creative clay session, I would have nothing more to sustain me than photos and fridge magnets.

I'm not convinced – as Krishnamurti seemed to be – that it is the dying who need comforting. If the rumors regarding an afterlife are true, then Winkie is now enjoying golden fields full of mice, and biding his time until I join him. If the worst comes to pass and there is no hereafter, then his consciousness left him that day in July, years ago, and he ceased to exist on *any* plane.

Either way, it is I who is burdened by the crushing weight of grief, chained to memories that only serve to remind me of how much was lost, and what I must live the rest of my days without. Cleveland Amory said it best when describing the grief he felt at the loss of his beloved cat Polar Bear: "It was not just that Polar Bear was not there. It was the awful overpowering weight of knowing that he would never ever be there again." Perhaps it should be the last task of the dying to comfort those he will leave behind.

My therapist once pondered the question of whether – knowing that the shorter lifespan of domestic pets guarantees eventual heartache – the relationship is *worth* that heartache. At the time, I was grieving the loss of a different cat, one who, in his final sickly year, took to joining me for a brief snuggle every night. He would lay half on my pillow and half on my chest, resting his head so close to mine that I could feel his small cat breath on my face, his cold wet nose on my cheek. It was this image that passed through my mind's eye as the shrink waxed philosophical, and I thought, *of course it's worth it – how could it be otherwise?*

I listen to George Harrison sing about wanting to see his Sweet Lord, and I understand now that "God" – whatever that may be – is not just some deity to aspire to seeing in the afterlife. He is here, *now,* in our passions, our convictions, our sorrow, and our joy. He is in the rain that ruins your good-hair day, and the breeze that caresses your cheek. He is in the dirt the gardener plays with, the quack of a happy duck, and the smile of a small grey tabby, and if we ignore all this in favor of some mythical day of rapture, then we have well and truly squandered a lifetime's-worth of opportunities to walk with Him.

This book has mirrored the contradictions in my heart: on the one hand, I grieve deeply and endlessly for those wonderful characters I have loved and lost, and on the other hand, I understand that to spend a lifetime mired in grief would be a waste. It *is* necessary to carry on, to love again – and again. To allow others into your heart, with the knowledge that they will never replace what you've lost, but they will certainly enhance your life, nonetheless.

This is the nature of healing, as well: to somehow salve the wounds of a painful childhood and learn to reach out, trust others, to *feel things* again with your heart and soul, after so many years of numbness and detachment. Researchers finally figured out what the rest of us already knew – that animals can help with that healing process, and indeed, the critter benefits are so profound that therapy dogs and cats are being pressed into service in hospital wards and nursing homes. Even EAP – Equine Assisted Psychotherapy – is now covered by some health insurance companies.

This is why I'm so passionate about kindness and respect for *all* animals, not just the cute and cuddly ones. They give us their unconditional love, they care when no one else seems to, and they do it because they choose to, not because they have to. There are some who may be classified as "rodents," or "pests," but they are all His creatures, and if there truly is a loving God, I don't believe he would appreciate the human members of his flock picking and choosing which animals to treat badly, and which to treat well.

These critters are also equally deserving of our awareness, if nothing else, that we have encroached on them dreadfully, and that we are unlikely to give back what we have taken from them: I've yet to see anyone tear down a strip mall in favor of creating a little critter habitat.

There was, in the roof of my chicken coop home, a small hole that I often saw a chipmunk disappear into. I was strongly advised by friends to seal up the hole before bad weather created serious problems. My first thought on hearing such advice was, *but what if the chipmunk's family gets trapped inside?* My second thought was, *I rent. What do I care if the roof has a small hole in it?* This may be a poor example for homeowners, but I saw no reason *not* to accommodate the chipmunk in some fashion; it's the least I could do.

It's heartbreaking to me to see how badly human-kind has handled the responsibility of caring for the earth, and its inhabitants, and I think that we *must* – if for no other reason than to redeem ourselves in His eyes – somehow make things right. Whether this means petitioning foreign powers to stop whaling, or fighting to save the Arctic National Wildlife Refuge from oil drilling, or just letting a chipmunk live in your roof, if we all make a small effort, then collectively, we'll really have something!

May all of you be as blessed by the love of great critters as I have been.

Kelly Meister is a writer, photographer, and potter. She shares her life with five cats, twelve ducks, and several ornery horses. Most mornings, Kelly can be found at McKinnon's pond, talking to those ducks and hoping no one overhears.

In her spare time, Kelly takes riding lessons, volunteers at a horse rescue facility, and waits on the cats hand and foot. She also donates her one-of-a-kind ceramic vases to animal charities for fund-raising purposes. If your critter charity would like one of Kelly's vases for your fund-raiser, or if you'd like Kelly to speak at your book club or other gathering, please email her at **K7lly@yahoo.com.**

Kelly hopes you'll visit **www.crazycritterlady.com** to meet the all the critters featured here.

Stay tuned for the next installment of *Crazy Critter* tales!

Epilogue